# Advance Praise for *Startup Campus*

"*Startup Campus* is a vital exploration of how leading universities like UC Berkeley are redefining their role in society. As someone whose work emerged from an ecosystem that values both fundamental science and entrepreneurial risk-taking, I see in this book a blueprint for the institutional evolution we need. Rich Lyons shows how universities can stay true to their academic core while becoming engines of innovation and impact. This is a must-read for anyone who believes in the power of science and education to change the world."

—JENNIFER DOUDNA, UC Berkeley biochemist, CRISPR pioneer and Nobel laureate, Innovative Genomics Institute founder

"UC Berkeley has shaped generations of tech pioneers—including me. *Startup Campus* distills the culture, policies, and spirit that made Berkeley a cradle of innovation, offering invaluable lessons for campuses everywhere."

—ERIC SCHMIDT, former CEO of Google and Executive Chairman of Alphabet Inc., co-author of *Genesis: Artificial Intelligence, Hope, and the Human Spirit*

"Berkeley has always been a place that fosters and honors scholars who can help us see the world around us in a wholly new way, those who turn conventional thinking upside down and make great intellectual leaps that change the world. Strangely, within Berkeley, that was once thought of as apart from entrepreneurial journeys beyond the academy. This book tells the marvelous story of how a few people shaped Berkeley's deliberate, rapid, and inspiring path to entrepreneurship excellence. It's a great story, and one that is sure to inspire other universities on their own journeys."

—PAUL ALIVISATOS, President, University of Chicago, pioneer in nanomaterials development

"*Startup Campus* demonstrates the power of the agile and scaled home for infinite creativity that UC Berkeley has become since the 1960s. This power has driven trillions of dollars of new economic energy and its replication is possible throughout the country by studying this fantastic American innovation story."

—MICHAEL M. CROW, President, Arizona State University, author of *The Fifth Wave: The Evolution of American Higher Education*

"Berkeley's entrepreneurial spirit transforms world-class research into real-world impact, advancing breakthroughs in human and environmental health. Supporting this engine of discovery means accelerating solutions for the challenges that define our time."

—BARBARA BASS BAKAR, former CEO for several major retail firms, founder of ACHIEVE, a high school scholarship and enrichment program

"UC Berkeley has been the home of revolutionary discoveries in science and technology for many decades. Sometimes less appreciated is how many of those have been translated into very successful products and companies across the digital, biotechnology, materials, chemistry, climate tech, and other sectors. This book is a must read for anyone interested in how visionary leadership built a campus entrepreneurship culture that spawned more venture capital funded startups than any other university."

—BROOK BYERS, cofounder of Kleiner Perkins and venture capital pioneer

"A key ingredient in the recipe for Silicon Valley and the US technology industry, is the critical role of the university. This book charts the evolution of UC Berkeley's enormous contribution and commitment to innovation and entrepreneurship that has fueled the growth of the technology industry, while maintaining its public mission and academic excellence. Berkeley's story is a valuable road map for every university to realize its potential to foster a culture of innovation and entrepreneurship that contributes to the improvement of our society and the student experience."

—LARRY W. SONSINI, Senior and Founding Partner of Wilson Sonsini

"I was there when entrepreneurship at Berkeley was still an experiment—before incubators, before venture labs. I watched a bold mix of academic rigor, risk-taking, and cross-disciplinary energy turn Berkeley into one of the world's engines for startups. This book captures that evolution and, for me, brings to life a personal journey that helped shape what academic innovation can become—a *Startup Campus.*"

—STEVE BLANK, serial entrepreneur and creator of the Lean Startup methodology

"Public universities are America's greatest innovation and there is no better example than Berkeley. It changed my life. Here's the story of how a great school also became a vital center of entrepreneurship."

—SCOTT GALLOWAY, Berkeley Haas 1992, Professor of Marketing, NYU Stern and Co-Host *Pivot* and *Prof G Markets* podcasts, serial entrepreneur

STARTUP CAMPUS

# STARTUP CAMPUS

**How UC Berkeley
Became an Unexpected Leader
in Entrepreneurship and Startups**

INNOVATION AND ENTREPRENEURSHIP COUNCIL
*University of California, Berkeley*

UC Berkeley Office of Innovation and Entrepreneurship
Berkeley, California

Every effort has been made to obtain permission to reproduce the graphics in this book. Please do get in touch with any inquiries or any information relating to any image.

ISBN 979-83487-0001-0 (cloth)
ISBN 979-83487-0002-7 (pbk.)
ISBN 979-83487-0003-4 (ebook)

# CONTENTS

Why and how does one of the world's oldest surviving institutions engage in and embrace quantum-leap change? What spurs an inherently conservative, risk-averse part of the establishment to chart a new course, to take on risk, to embrace innovation? This book provides compelling answers to those fascinating questions in the course of what is a historic phase-change story, one that applies to institutions with extraordinary societal impact: our universities.

The higher education sector has been around for centuries. The University of Bologna dates to 1088. Harvard is 140 years older than the United States. The list of long-lived universities is not only impressive, it's also remarkably different from and often compared to the relatively short-lived enterprises in the economic sphere (over the past 40 years, more than one-third of companies in the S&P 500 have been replaced during the average ten-year period). Along with that stability there has been a degree of stagnation.

None of this is to say that universities haven't changed; they certainly have. New disciplines have been embraced. New financial models have been implemented. The role of alumni has taken on great significance. Public universities in the United States have dramatically changed the demographic mix of students since Abraham Lincoln launched the land-grant system in 1862.

Now, however, I believe we're seeing something completely

different. Universities were traditionally seen as ivory towers, places for professors to pursue knowledge for its own sake. Today, the society we serve expects more, and needs more than the basic academic research we have excelled at for so long. The world is increasingly turning to our universities in pursuit of tangible ideas, innovations, and solutions that will advance the greater good. I refer to this concept as the "generative university."

*Startup Campus* delves deeply into the transformation that is well underway at UC Berkeley, and to varying degrees at many other universities—a transformation that is already delivering valuable outcomes for society. In recent years we have, at Berkeley, significantly boosted our support for innovation and entrepreneurship. New classes. New programs. New approaches. New outcomes. For example, few readers might know that Berkeley undergraduate alumni have founded more venture capital–funded businesses than those from any other university in the world, and the results of this remarkable addition to our institutional ethos and impact are both wide and deep. As research by Berkeley's own Professor Emmanuel Saez shows (see his National Bureau of Economic Research working paper with Raj Chetty), this success in fostering entrepreneurship and translational research contributes directly to Berkeley's record of lifting more people further up the household income ladder, from one generation to the next, than any other top university.

As you will learn, universities' expanding societal impact is not just about startups and lifting people socioeconomically. Imagine, for instance, a world without UC Berkeley. No cancer immunotherapy. No CRISPR gene editing. No understanding of dark matter and the accelerating universe.

What this book does is pull back the covers on the remarkable evolution and adaptation of universities like UC Berkeley as their campuses are animated by new promise and potential. In these pages is an exploration of the extent to which transformative change can beget a wide array of profound consequences for the campus's students, staff, and faculty, not to mention the nature and extent of the institution's impact on the world beyond the campus. Opportunities beget opportunities.

Make no mistake, change also involves unintended consequences, and this book doesn't shy away from a clear-eyed comprehensive look, if only because opportunities also beget challenges and inherent tensions. For example, are translational research and fundamental research in conflict? Or, as economists like me tend to frame it, are they complements or substitutes? If, let's say, a startup-rich campus pulls the world's best researchers away from fundamental research, that would be a consequence of great cost to society. What lies ahead in these pages are encouraging and surprising examples of how our university is carefully and successfully navigating waters that remain largely uncharted.

I also believe that the publication of *Startup Campus* could not be more timely. Societal trust and confidence in higher education are at a historic low, even as it's increasingly evident that the public's awareness and understanding of what modern universities are doing and contributing have not caught up with the breadth and depth of the change described in this book. This is understandable since major change has occurred in a relatively short time frame, not just at Berkeley but across many universities worldwide.

I may be a bit biased, but here before you is a thrilling, inspiring story of an exemplary university on the rise at a time of both peril and potential. The stakes are high. The time is right, and this is an insightful, thought-provoking read.

Richard K. Lyons
Chancellor, University of California, Berkeley

## 2024 startup rankings

| | University | Founder count | Company count |
|---|---|---|---|
| **1** | **UC Berkeley** | **1,811** | **1,642** |
| 2 | Stanford | 1,547 | 1,397 |
| 3 | Harvard | 1,352 | 1,222 |
| 4 | University of Pennsylvania | 1,197 | 1,099 |
| 5 | MIT | 1,175 | 1,049 |

Source: PitchBook

UC Berkeley is the top university in number of venture capital–funded companies founded by undergraduate alumni. (SOURCE: NEIL FREESE/UC BERKELEY)

# INTRODUCTION

From revolutionary digital technology and biotech startups to pioneering climate tech ventures, UC Berkeley has emerged as an unexpected leader in innovation and entrepreneurship (I&E).[1] This transformation is remarkable for a public university that once viewed involvement with corporations with skepticism. The birthplace of the 1960s Free Speech Movement has reinvented itself in ways that have advanced the university's mission of research, education, and public service. Today, Berkeley's I&E ecosystem offers a model for how universities with a mandate to drive social mobility can tackle the world's pressing issues and power economic vitality.[2] Berkeley's journey to I&E excellence illuminates a future for higher education in the twenty-first century.

1. In September 2024, according to data from PitchBook, UC Berkeley was ranked the top university in (1) venture-funded startups founded by undergraduate alumni, (2) venture-funded startups founded by female alumnae, and (3) capital raised by female alumnae. Jason Pohl, "UC Berkeley Ranked No. 1 for Generating Startup Founders, Companies, and Female Entrepreneurs," *UC Berkeley News,* September 4, 2024, https://news.berkeley.edu/2024/09/04/uc-berkeley-ranked-no-1-for-generating-startup-founders-companies-and-female-entrepreneurs/.

2. An I&E ecosystem is a term of art for a geographically dense cluster of people, programs, and institutions that foster (1) an entrepreneurial mindset, (2) the creation and growth of scalable startup enterprises, and (3) the proliferation of innovations that improve the quality of life and economic vitality of a region and the world.

However, Berkeley's transformation over the years into an I&E leader wasn't inevitable. This change sparked controversy and encountered resistance. Even today, the campus grapples with multiple challenges. These include the risk that an increasing emphasis on applied research and societal impact will weaken Berkeley's preeminence in fundamental science, dilute its public mission, or distort its academic culture.[3] The stakes are high. How Berkeley navigates this balance offers insights for research universities worldwide.

*Startup Campus* tells the inside story of the origins and rise of Berkeley's I&E ecosystem from the perspective of faculty, staff, and alumni who have led the campus's transformation. What drove Berkeley's I&E surge? How has the university leveraged its I&E success? What can other universities with unrealized I&E aspirations learn from Berkeley? Those questions and more are examined in this book.[4]

There isn't a single formula for building a university's I&E ecosystem because no two universities are the same—as exemplified by Berkeley's unique combination of campus culture, academic breadth, and geographic attributes. Each campus has characteristics that offer varying I&E opportunities. Nonetheless, most universities share common attributes, such as cutting-edge research, inspiring courses, expert faculty, ambitious students, experienced staff, and loyal alumni. This book reveals how Berkeley has leveraged those common elements to

3. According to the 2024 ranking by *US News and World Report*, some thirty Berkeley graduate programs rank in the top ten.

4. This book is focused on UC Berkeley's I&E excellence and therefore doesn't cover the many other aspects of UC Berkeley excellence, such as scholarly research, socioeconomic mobility, extraordinary philanthropists, and socially responsible licensing. In addition, this book isn't about how to launch and grow startups or how to be an entrepreneur.

maximize its I&E impact and how other universities can realize their I&E potential.

*Startup Campus* is organized into seven chapters. The first six chapters segment Berkeley's I&E ecosystem development into six phases, each with a progressive series of accomplishments and conflicts. The final chapter offers strategic takeaways gleaned from Berkeley's I&E journey. Interwoven throughout the chapters are stories of how Berkeley founders spun out startup ventures and leveraged the campus's resources.

Chapter 1 opens with the origins of Berkeley's I&E culture starting in the late 1960s and its seminal relationship to the early digital technology and biotech industries. Despite phenomenal success, the pockets of Berkeley's I&E culture maintained a low profile during those years. Conflicts with the prevailing ideology were exemplified by the expectation that any financial gains from faculty research should accrue to the state and the university rather than the inventors because taxpayers paid their salaries.[5]

Chapter 2 covers Berkeley's I&E development from 2000 through 2006. During this period the university's budget strains motivated it to pursue research collaborations with industry. Those collaborations laid the groundwork for the coming embrace of startups. However, it pitted a growing reliance on industry-funded research against potential industry constraints on academic freedom.

Chapter 3 describes a sequence of foundational initiatives from 2007 through 2012 that put Berkeley on a trajectory toward

5. Martin Kenney and W. Richard Goe, "The Role of Social Embeddedness in Professorial Entrepreneurship: A Comparison of Electrical Engineering and Computer Science at UC Berkeley and Stanford," *Research Policy* 33, no. 5 (July 2024): 691–707, 696.

I&E ascendence. The potential of providing solutions to the planet's calamitous environmental situation combined with the benefits of student experiential learning overcame objections to the increasing involvement with industry and societal impact.

Chapter 4 highlights a six-year boom in Berkeley's I&E growth from 2013 through 2018 that exploded its capacity. A groundswell of STEM student interest in entrepreneurship motivated faculty and staff in different departments to launch new I&E programs. This decentralized, unfettered ecosystem growth raised the issue of whether uncoordinated exuberance resulted in suboptimal outcomes for the campus.

Chapter 5 details how the campus harmonized, expanded, and raised the visibility of its I&E ecosystem beginning in 2019 and continuing through 2024. Equally important, the campus leadership addressed a simmering entrepreneurial cultural rift between Berkeley's STEM community and its humanities and social sciences communities.

Chapter 6 highlights Berkeley's I&E plans for 2025 and beyond. Those plans articulate a vision for the expanding importance of I&E at universities, while continuing the unwavering pursuit of fundamental research, teaching excellence, and social mobility.

Chapter 7 reframes how Berkeley became an I&E powerhouse and offers strategic takeaways that can inform how other universities can pursue their full I&E potential.

*Startup Campus* has an accompanying website (startupcam pus.berkeley.edu) that delves deeper into Berkeley's I&E ecosystem, provides the latest ecosystem updates, and enables founders who have spun out companies from Berkeley to submit their startup stories to the website.

# ONE

# Incubating an Entrepreneurship Culture

The value of an idea lies in the using of it.

—■ THOMAS ALVA EDISON

## Berkeley I&E, 1960s–2000

In the mid-twentieth century, pockets of UC Berkeley faculty and students were at the forefront of the early digital technology and biotechnology industries. These industries created the first markets in which startup companies and venture capital flourished. The success of startup companies and venture capital investments inspired those Berkeley professors and students to trailblaze a campus culture that valued the societal use of their innovations. In addition to educating students, publishing papers, and consulting for corporations, these professors also founded companies and extolled the virtues of entrepreneurship.[1]

However, Berkeley's nascent startup culture remained siloed during this period, partly because at the time entrepreneurship wasn't considered in faculty appointments or promotions.[2] In

1. University of California faculty are allowed to consult professionally for third-party organizations one day per week.

2. Recognition of I&E accomplishments in faculty promotions and appointments was officially changed at UC Berkeley in 2018, and for the entire

fact, some professors effectively hid their startup activities because of a prevailing campus mindset that entrepreneurship (1) wasn't consistent with scholarship and was associated with a profit motive that should be distinct from a university's mission, and (2) detracted from time that faculty could devote to research and department service, which wasn't a moral judgment but a pragmatic observation.[3]

Berkeley's founding in 1868 as a land grant institution and constitutionally designated public trust also contributed to the general campus disdain for faculty involvement in commercial endeavors.[4] During these formative years a manifestation of that attitude was the feeling of superiority that professors in the so-called pure fields had over their colleagues in the applied fields (such as agriculture and engineering).[5]

Despite that ethos, Berkeley's early entrepreneurs were driven in part by the immense value that society could gain from their innovations. From the late 1960s through the 1990s, startup companies with Berkeley founders helped create several new industries. These include the following:

- **Microprocessors.** Intel was cofounded in 1968 by Berkeley undergraduate alumnus Gordon Moore and Berkeley chemical engineering PhD alumnus Andrew Grove.

---

University of California system in April 2022; see UC Board of Regents "Policy of Innovation Transfer & Entrepreneurship," iande.berkeley.edu/sites/default/files/recognizing_innovation_transfer_and_entrepreneurship_in_the_academic_personnel_process.pdf .

3. "Entrepreneurship at Berkeley," 2018 report, page 28.

4. "Shared Governance at the University of California," Berkeley Public Policy, Goldman School, gspp.berkeley.edu/research-and-impact/publications/shared-governance-at-the-university-of-california-an-historical-review.

5. Kenney and Goe, "Role of Social Embeddedness in Professorial Entrepreneurship," 691–707, 696.

- **Personal computers.** Apple was cofounded in 1976 by former Berkeley undergraduate Steve Wozniak.

- **Biotechnology.**

  - Cetus was cofounded in 1971 by Berkeley professor (and winner of the 1960 Nobel Prize in Physics) Donald Glaser and Berkeley postdoctoral fellow Ronald Cape. Chiron acquired Cetus for $300 million in 1991.

  - Chiron was cofounded in 1981 by Berkeley biochemistry professor Edward Penhoet. Novartis acquired Chiron for $5 billion in 2005.

- **Structural and earthquake engineering software.** Computers and Structures, Inc. was founded in 1975 by Berkeley civil engineering alumnus Ashraf Habibullah.

- **Relational databases.**

  - Relational Technology was cofounded in 1980 by Berkeley electrical engineering and computer science professors Michael Stonebraker and Eugene Wong. Relational changed its name to Ingres and went public in 1988.

  - Informix was founded in 1980 by Berkeley undergraduate alumnus Roger Sippl. IBM acquired Informix for $1 billion in 2001.

  - Sybase was cofounded in 1984 by Berkeley electrical engineering and computer science PhD Robert Epstein. SAP acquired Sybase for $5.8 billion in 2010.

- **Networked computing.** Sun Microsystems was cofounded in 1982 by Berkeley electrical engineering and computer science alumnus Bill Joy. Oracle acquired Sun for $6 billion in 2009.

## Bio-Rad Labs: First Berkeley Startup

Bio-Rad Laboratories is among Berkeley's first successful spinout companies, and it's still thriving as of 2025.[a] It was founded by two Berkeley undergraduate alumni, Alice and David Schwartz, who both received chemistry degrees. After graduating, they married and cofounded Bio-Rad in 1952. The name Bio-Rad comes from the words *biochemicals* and *radiochemicals*, the company's first products.

The Schwartzes opened their first laboratory in a 1,600-square-foot Quonset hut in Berkeley with just $720 in savings. By 1960, Bio-Rad's operations in biological discovery and health-care research had expanded to eleven employees and $150,000 in sales. In 1966 the company reached $1 million in annual sales and became a publicly traded company. As of 2024, Bio-Rad had seventy-eight hundred employees and $2.5 billion in annual sales of life science research tools and clinical diagnostics.

For more than seventy years Bio-Rad products and systems have provided clinical information for blood transfusions,

- ▪ **Electronic design automation.** Cadence Design Systems (see the sidebar in this chapter) was cofounded in 1983 by Berkeley MSEE alumnus James Solomon, along with Berkeley electrical engineering and computer science professors Alberto Sangiovanni-Vincentelli and Richard Newton.[6]

6. Richard Newton was the dean of the College of Engineering from 2000 until his untimely death in 2007. In addition to cofounding Cadence, Newton was a venture capital partner and the lead advocate for CITRIS, the Center for Information Technology Research in the Interest of Society (profiled in chapter 2).

In 1952, David and Alice Schwartz began Bio-Rad in a 1,600-square-foot Quonset hut in Berkeley, California (COURTESY OF BIO-RAD LABS)

diabetes monitoring, and autoimmune and infectious disease testing. These products have helped advance the discovery process in research labs around the world and support the diagnosis, monitoring, and treatment of diseases and other medical conditions. ▪

a. The first documented commercialization of a technology developed by a UC Berkeley professor was in 1907, when Frederick Cottrell invented an electrostatic precipitator. Cottrell believed that the university shouldn't participate in business, and there wasn't a university policy regarding faculty inventions. So Cottrell founded the Research Corporation to commercialize his invention. Source: Kenney and Goe, "Role of Social Embeddedness in Professorial Entrepreneurship."

▪ **Quantitative investing.** Renaissance Technologies and its Medallion Fund was founded in the 1980s by Berkeley PhD James Simons.

▪ **Energy bars.** PowerBar was founded in 1985 by Berkeley undergraduate alumnus Brian Maxwell.

▪ **Data storage and networking controller market.** Marvell Technologies was cofounded in 1995 by Berkeley alumni Sehat Sutardja, Weili Dai, and Pantas Sutardja.

▪ **Internet search and content delivery market.** Inktomi was cofounded in 1996 by Berkeley electrical engineering and computer science professors Eric Brewer and Paul Gauthier. Yahoo acquired Inktomi for $241 million in 2002.

■ **Enterprise software for learning and talent management.** Saba Software was founded in 1997 by Berkeley undergraduate alumnus Bobby Yazdani and first employee Berkeley undergraduate alumnus Grant Ricketts.

During this period at Berkeley, except for the Department of Electrical Engineering and Computer Science (EECS), faculty and students with an entrepreneurial mindset were scattered and isolated around the campus—for example, in the chemistry-related departments and the Haas School of Business.[7] The business school offered a class on entrepreneurship in the 1970s and in 1991 launched an extracurricular program focused on entrepreneurship and startups called the Lester Center for Entrepreneurship (profiled later in this chapter).

However, the EECS department had a growing cadre of entrepreneurial and commercially minded professors and students, many with offices in Cory Hall's legendary fifth floor (added to the building in 1985 and funded by corporations to pursue cutting-edge digital technology research). In the final years of the twentieth century, the future of this embryonic cluster of Berkeley's I&E culture was uncertain. Would it (1) be drummed out by the public university's norms, (2) maintain its siloed low profile to not attract a backlash from those norms, or (3) expand to become a change agent of campus norms and a driving force of Berkeley's I&E excellence? *(continued on page 14)*

---

7. The Law and Economics Consulting Group was incorporated as the LECG Corporation in 1988 and founded by Berkeley School of Business professor David Teece. Teknekron Corporation, a contract research firm and technology product incubator, was cofounded in 1968 by several Berkeley faculty, including EECS professor George Turin.

# Cadence Design Systems: Making Modern Digital Technology Possible

Digital technology has had a pervasive and profound impact on our world. The technology's impact was made possible by squeezing billions of electronic components (e.g., transistors) of nanometric size onto little integrated circuits—also known as chips. However, the design and fabrication of those chips would not be possible without the use of computer-based design tools. Alberto Luigi Sangiovanni-Vincentelli, a UC Berkeley professor of electrical engineering and computer science, was at the forefront of inventing those design tools and launching the electronic design automation (EDA) industry (also known as ECAD, or electronic computer-aided design).

In 1975, Alberto came to Berkeley as a young engineer from Milan, Italy. At that time semiconductor-integrated circuit chips were largely designed manually by specialized engineers. The design process was laborious, error-prone, time-consuming, and consequently resulted in expensive chips with limited functionality.

At Berkeley, Alberto focused his research on optimization algorithms for designing chips. It was an exciting time for the promising nascent field of EDA, and Berkeley was at its fore-

UC Berkeley professor Sangiovanni-Vincentelli and his family after they moved to Berkeley in 1976 (COURTESY OF ALBERTO SANGIOVANNI-VINCENTELLI)

front. That enabled Alberto and his faculty colleagues to raise funds from companies to build an entire floor on top of Cory Hall (initially built in 1950) dedicated to research on computer-based tools for chip design, testing, and fabrication. The exterior of the new top floor features a computer chip–inspired architectural motif.

During that period Alberto, along with his postdocs and graduate students, developed computer simulation tools, hardware description languages, and component arrangement methodologies that accelerated chip design, optimized chip performance, and minimized power consumption. Alberto and his Berkeley colleagues were firm believers in putting the advancement of knowledge and societal impact above their economic interests. Accordingly, they made their EDA innovations

UC Berkeley professor Alberto Sangiovanni-Vincentelli (COURTESY OF ALBERTO SANGIOVANNI-VINCENTELLI)

freely available (instead of requiring royalty-bearing patent and software licenses).

To help market his innovations and apply them to the specific needs of individual digital technology companies, Alberto cofounded Cadence Design Systems in 1983 with Berkeley EECS professor Richard Newton and Berkeley alumnus James Solomon. Four years later, Alberto cofounded Synopsys, another EDA company. Both companies have grown into multinationals that employ tens of thousands of people. As of 2023, EDA was a $16 billion industry.

Alberto won the Foundation Frontiers of Knowledge Award in Information and Communication Technologies in 2023. The award committee cited him for "radically transforming" the design of the chips that power today's electronic devices, leading to "the modern semiconductor industry" and creating "a rich ecosystem of electronic design automation (EDA) techniques that revolutionized—and remain at the core of—how we build computer systems." In addition to Alberto's scientific achievements, he cofounded Cadence and Synopsys, which "collectively drive the entire semiconductor industry," the committee added.[a]

As of 2024, Alberto was still serving on the board of Cadence, which he describes as "like one of my children."[b] He also supports Berkeley's entrepreneurship community in many ways, most notably as an advisor to Berkeley's SkyDeck startup accelerator (profiled in chapters 3 and 4) with a special emphasis on SkyDeck's chip track and SkyDeck Europe Milano program. ▪

a. BBVA Foundation, "Frontiers of Knowledge Awards," www.frontiersof knowledgeawards-fbbva.es/noticias/15th-edition-information-communica tion-technologies-alberto-sangiovanni-vincentelli/

b. BBVA Foundation, "Frontiers of Knowledge Awards," www.frontiersof knowledgeawards-fbbva.es/noticias/15th-edition-information-communica tion-technologies-alberto-sangiovanni-vincentelli/

## Digital Technology Revolution

Starting in the 1960s and 1970s, UC Berkeley's Department of Electrical Engineering and Computer Science (EECS) was instrumental in the formation of the digital technology revolution and its many market sectors that catalyzed the venture capital industry and the proliferation of the startup business model.

However, the department's technological advancements alone didn't spearhead the digital technology sectors. Equally important was a culture among a cadre of professors and students in the department who valued the commercialization of their innovations, collaborations with companies, and a spirit of entrepreneurship. That culture of entrepreneurship was likely inspired, at least partially, by the rise of successful startup companies only about fifty miles south of Berkeley in what became known as Silicon Valley.

The EECS department exhibited its commercialization mindset by encouraging the free use of its new technology under a license agreement pioneered at Berkeley called the BSD (Berkeley Software Distribution) open-source license agreement. This revolutionary license contrasted with the conventional approach of requiring companies to execute a royalty-bearing license agreement before they could commercialize a university's patented technology or copyrighted software. Notable examples of the EECS department's open-sourced innovations that propelled digital technology industries in the late twentieth century include the following:

- In 1973 the integrated circuit design software called SPICE (Simulation Program with Integrated Circuit Emphasis) led to the creation of the electronic design automation industry and new companies such as Cadence Design Systems in 1983 (see the sidebar in this chapter) and Synopsys in 1987.

Cory Hall, home of the UC Berkeley EECS Department with its fifth-floor addition and integrated circuit architectural motif

- In the mid-1970s through the mid-1980s, the relational database project called Ingres (Interactive Graphics Retrieval System) led to the launch of several relational database companies, including Relational Technology (Ingres), Informix, and Sybase.

- In 1978 the computer operating system called Berkeley UNIX (Uniplexed Information Computing System) led to the founding of Sun Microsystems in 1983, one of the pioneers of the networked-computing workstation and server industry. Berkeley UNIX was the first example of a large-scale open-source software project at a university. It demonstrated the potential of an open environment for innovation, paving the way for later successful projects such as Linux.[8]

8. Richard Karp, "A Personal View of Computer Science at Berkeley," 2003, www2.eecs.berkeley.edu/bears/CS_Anniversary/karp-talk.html.

■ In the early 1980s seminal advances in computer micro-processor architecture, coined RISC (Reduced Instruction Set Computer) by Berkeley professors, accelerated the high-performance computer industry and led to startups such as MIPS Computer Systems and SiFive, cofounded in 2015 by Berkeley professor Krste Asanović and Berkeley PhDs Yunsup Lee and Andrew Waterman.

■ In 1987 the data storage virtualization technology called RAID (Redundant Array of Inexpensive Disks) revolutionized the cost and performance of computer disk drives. That helped propel the computer industry and inspired startups such as Network Appliance (later renamed NetApp), cofounded in 1992 by Berkeley undergraduate alumnus James Lau.

■ Leveraging the advances in microelectromechanical sys-tems (MEMS) and wireless connectivity, a team of Berkeley EECS researchers in the late 1990s developed TinyOS, an open-source operating system for wireless sensor networks. These networks consist of low-power, miniature, single-chip sensors that can scale to networks of thousands of sensor nodes. TinyOS research was the precursor to modern ubiquitous sensor networks, which led to startups such as Crossbow Technology founded in 1995 by Berkeley under-graduate Mike Horton and Dust Networks founded in 2002 by Berkeley professor Kris Pister.

Beyond open-sourcing software, Berkeley EECS researchers spearheaded other digital technology sectors during this peri-od.[9] These include semiconductor design and manufacturing

9. For more detail on the history of the Department of Electrical Engineering and Computer Science at UC Berkeley, see "History," eecs.berkeley.edu/about/history.

(facilitated by the 1983 opening of the Microlab on the fourth floor of Cory Hall) as well as the following sectors:

▪ **Microelectromechanical systems (MEMS).** In the early 1980s, Berkeley researchers achieved a breakthrough by fabricating mechanical elements with integrated circuits on a single chip. That enabled the use of MEMS for many applications, including automobiles, smartphones, and gas and chemical sensors. In 1986 the US National Science Foundation funded a government-university-industry research collaboration called the Berkeley Sensor and Actuator Center (BSAC). BSAC's foundational vision was that miniaturization in any technological domain—whether electrical, mechanical, chemical, or biological—leads to compelling performance benefits. BSAC research led to several MEMS startups, including Berkeley Lights (profiled in chapter 3), Chirp Microsystems (profiled in chapter 4), Iota Biosciences (profiled in chapter 5), Discera cofounded in 2001 by Berkeley professor Clark Nguyen, and Silicon Clocks cofounded in 2006 by Berkeley professor Roger Howe and Berkeley postdoctoral fellow Emmanuel Quevy.

▪ **Wireless connectivity.** In 1995, Berkeley EECS professors envisioned a world with ubiquitous connectivity using wireless technology. That led to the 1999 launch of the Berkeley Wireless Research Center. This university-industry-government partnership takes a systems approach to pioneering circuits and system-on-chip innovations for high-performance analog, digital, and mixed-signal wireless and wireline applications.

In the twenty-first century the EECS department expanded on its track record of technology leadership, open-sourcing intellectual property, and spinning out startups by way of a series of five-year collaborative research labs. These included:

- RADLab (2005–10) focused on the emergence of cloud computing. The RADLab inspired such startups as Conviva, cofounded in 2006 by Berkeley professor Ion Stoica and Berkeley PhD Hui Zhang; Cloudera, cofounded in 2008 by Berkeley alumnus Mike Horton; and Nicira Networks, cofounded in 2007 by Berkeley professor Scott Shenker and Berkeley PhD Nick McKeown. VMWare acquired Nicira in 2012 for $1.26 billion.

- AMPLab (2011–16) focused on big data analytics. The AMPLab developed and open-sourced Apache Spark, which led to the startup Databricks, cofounded in 2013 by Berkeley professors Ali Ghodsi and Ion Stoica.

- RISELab (2017–22) focused on real-time intelligence. The RISELab developed and open-sourced Ray, which led to the startup Anyscale, cofounded in 2019 by Berkeley professor Ion Stoica and Berkeley PhDs Philipp Moritz and Robert Nishihara.

- Berkeley AI Research (BAIR) launched in 2023, bringing together researchers in computer vision, machine learning, natural language processing, planning, control, and robotics. As of 2024, BAIR included over fifty faculty and more than three hundred graduate students and postdoctoral fellows pursuing research on fundamental advances in the above areas as well as cross-cutting themes including multimodal deep learning, human-compatible AI, and connecting AI with other scientific disciplines and the humanities.

AI research at Berkeley has led to the following startups:

- OpenAI, cofounded in 2015 by Berkeley PhD John Schulman.
- Covariant, cofounded in 2017 by Berkeley professor Pieter Abbeel and Berkeley PhDs Peter Chen, Rocky Duan, and Tianhao Zhang.
- Ambi Robotics, cofounded in 2018 by Berkeley professor Ken Goldberg; Berkeley PhDs Jeff Mahler, Matthew Matl, and Stephen McKinley; and Berkeley undergraduate David Gealy.
- Perplexity, cofounded in 2022 by Berkeley PhD Aravind Srinivas.
- Jacobi Robotics, cofounded in 2022 by Berkeley professor Ken Goldberg; Berkeley postdoctoral fellow Jeff Ichnowski; Berkeley PhD Yahav Avigal; and Berkeley alumnus Max Cao.
- Skild AI, cofounded in 2023 by Berkeley PhD Deepak Pathak.
- Physical Intelligence, cofounded in 2024 by Berkeley professor Sergey Levine and Berkeley PhD Chelsea Finn.

## Biotechnology Revolution

The biotech industry was born in the San Francisco Bay Area in 1976 with the launch of Genentech, the first genetic engineering company, and for the next thirty years UC Berkeley was one of five research institutions (along with UC San Francisco, UC San Diego, Stanford, and Scripps) responsible for two-thirds of the six hundred biotech companies in California by the turn of the

UC Berkeley Weill Hall houses forty-six laboratories for advanced biological research

century.[10] Trailblazing biotech companies with Berkeley roots during this period included the following:

- Cetus was cofounded in 1971 by Berkeley physics professor (and winner of the 1960 Nobel Prize in Physics) Donald Glaser and Berkeley postdoctoral fellow Ronald Cape. Cetus merged in 1991 with Chiron.

- Chiron was cofounded in 1981 by Berkeley biochemistry professor Edward Penhoet.

- Tularik was cofounded in 1991 by Berkeley professor Robert Tjian. Amgen acquired Tularik for $1.3 billion in 2004.

- Exelixis was cofounded in 1994 by Berkeley professors Corey Goodman and Gerry Rubin.

10. According to "California's Biomedical Industry," 2004 report, PriceWaterhouseCooper.

■ Acacia Biosciences was cofounded in 1995 by Berkeley professor Jasper Rine and Berkeley postdoctoral fellow Randy Hampton. Acacia merged in 1999 with Rosetta Inpharmatics and was acquired in 2001 by Merck for an undisclosed amount.

■ Sunesis Pharmaceuticals was cofounded in 1998 by Berkeley chemistry professor Jonathan Ellman.

As mentioned, in the previous century, beyond the pockets of I&E at Berkeley, most faculty were apathetic or even averse to the commercialization of technology developed at the campus. That widespread mindset was memorialized in a 1998 oral history about the early biotechnology industry with Berkeley biochemistry professor Ed Penhoet, cofounder of Chiron in 1981.[11] Penhoet stated:

> Certainly there always was a negative view about commercial activities on the Berkeley campus, maybe more pronounced than in most places...

> The sixties and seventies were periods where there was a big chasm between business and academia. It developed over the politics of the sixties. There was deep mistrust on both sides of that chasm. Berkeley was always identified as being one of the most leftist places in the country. Whether it truly was or not is another matter. So I think there was a general distrust of business and business people on campus...

11. "Regional Characteristics of Biotechnology in the United States: Perspectives of Three Industry Insiders," oral histories with Hugh A. Dt Andrade, David P. Holveck, and Edward E. Penhoet conducted in 1998 and 1999 by Sally Smith Hughes, Regional Oral History Office, The Bancroft Library, University of California, Berkeley, 2001.

That oral history was recorded in 1998, and in response to the interviewer's question "Opinion has swung 180 degrees, hasn't it?" Penhoet simply responded, "Yes." This succinctly captured the magnitude of Berkeley's I&E cultural transformation.

In the early 2000s Berkeley's departments of chemistry and biological sciences continued their track record of technology leadership and spinning out startups, as exemplified by the following companies:

- Plexxikon was cofounded in 2001 by Berkeley chemistry professor Sung-Hou Kim. The Japanese pharmaceutical company Daiichi Sankyo acquired Plexxikon in 2011 for $900 million.

- Renovis was cofounded in 2001 by Berkeley professor Corey Goodman. Evotec acquired Renovis in 2008 for $150 million.

- Ambryx was cofounded in 2003 by Berkeley professor Peter Schultz. Johnson & Johnson acquired Ambryx in 2024 for $3 billion.

- Aduro Biotech was founded in 2008 by Berkeley undergraduate alumnus Stephen Isaacs. Aduro went public in 2015, merged with Chinook Therapeutics in 2020, and the combined company was acquired by Novartis in 2023 for $3.5 billion.

- Carmot Therapeutics was cofounded in 2008 by Berkeley postdoctoral fellow Stig Hansen. Roche acquired Carmot in 2023 for about $3 billion.

- Redwood Bioscience was cofounded in 2008 by Berkeley professor (and winner of the 2022 Nobel Prize in Chemistry) Carolyn Bertozzi and Berkeley PhD David Rabuka. Catalent Pharma acquired Redwood in 2014 for an undisclosed amount.

- Nurix Therapeutics was cofounded in 2009 by Berkeley professors Michael Rape and John Kuriyan.

- Valitor was cofounded in 2010 by Berkeley professors Kevin Healy and David Schaffer, and Berkeley PhD Wesley Jackson.

- Caribou Biosciences (profiled in chapter 3) was cofounded in 2011 by Berkeley professor (and winner of the 2020 Nobel Prize in Chemistry) Jennifer Doudna and Berkeley PhD Rachel Haurwitz.

- Luciera Health was cofounded in 2013 by Berkeley PhDs Debkishora Mitra and John Waldeisen. Pfizer acquired Luciera in 2023 for an undisclosed amount.

- Rewrite Therapeutics was founded in 2016 by Berkeley PhD Shakked Halperin and Berkeley professor David Schaffer. Rewrite changed its name from Evolve Biotech and was acquired in 2022 by Intellia Therapeutics for $200 million.

- Vedere Bio was cofounded in 2019 by Berkeley professors John Flannery and Ehud Isacoff. Novartis acquired Vedere in 2020 for $150 million.

- Eikon Therapeutics was cofounded in 2019 by Berkeley professors Eric Betzig (winner of the 2014 Nobel Prize in Chemistry), Xavier Darzacq, and Robert Tijan.

## First Berkeley Program for Entrepreneurship and Startups

Despite the series of trailblazing startups with Berkeley origins in the 1970s and 1980s, it wasn't until 1991 that the first Berkeley program with a focus on entrepreneurship and startups was established as the Lester Center for Entrepreneurship in Berke-

**ENTREPRENEURSHIP**
▨▨▨▨▨▨▨▨ BERKELEY HAAS

ley's Haas School of Business.[12] Led by its inaugural executive director, Jerome (Jerry) Engel, the Lester Center orchestrated three programs that spearheaded Berkeley's I&E growth:

- **UC Berkeley Entrepreneurs Forum.** This program featured a networking hour followed by a presentation on a topic of interest to undergraduate and graduate students, venture capitalists, and members of related professional organizations.

- **Entrepreneurial Best Practices Series.** This series was designed to help entrants to the UC Berkeley Startup Competition and the Global Social Venture Competition develop their novel business ideas.

- **Richard Newton Distinguished Innovator Lecture Series/ Life as an Entrepreneur Series.** This lecture series featured distinguished entrepreneurs from organizations at various stages of development and representing a broad range of industries.

The Lester Center also operated a space in the basement of the Bancroft Hotel (located on the southern border of Berkeley's core campus) for Berkeley entrepreneurs and their startups to set up their initial offices. That space incubated such startups as TubeMogul, which was cofounded by Berkeley MBA students Brett Wilson and John Hughes. TubeMogul had an initial public offering in 2014 and was acquired by Adobe Systems in 2016 for approximately $549 million.

---

12. The Lester Center for Entrepreneurship was made possible by philanthropic funding from W. Howard Lester.

Berkeley Haas School of Business

In 2016 the Lester Center was expanded and rebranded as the Berkeley-Haas Entrepreneurship Program. As of 2025, the program's resources continue to thrive as key spokes in Berkeley's I&E ecosystem.

# TWO

# Embracing Collaborations with Companies

Innovation is the ability to see change as an opportunity, not a threat.

—■ STEVE JOBS

## Berkeley I&E, 2000–2006

The onset of the twenty-first century marked a turning point in industry collaborations for UC Berkeley and the entire ten-campus University of California system. Under the direction of California governor Gray Davis, the university established multicampus partnerships with industry to fund research as well as drive economic development and societal impact. This shift was critical to innovation and entrepreneurship at Berkeley because it legitimized clusters of faculty culture that valued collaborations with corporations and eventually fostered a broader campus culture that embraced collaborations with startup companies.

During the 1990s the State of California's funding for the University of California (UC) fell from over 70 percent to below 60 percent of the budget, and that downward trend was expected to continue.[1] In 2000, motivated in large part to offset the state's decreased

1. UC Academic Council, "Current Budget Trends and the Future of the

UC funding with financial support from the numerous successful innovative companies based in California, the governor launched four industry-UC partnerships called Institutes for Science and Innovation. Each institute spanned multiple UC campuses, and two of them incorporated the Berkeley campus: the California Institute for Quantitative Biosciences (QB3) and the Center for Information Technology Research in the Interest of Society (CITRIS).[2]

Though the UC system embraced industry collaborations, corporate involvement in university research was controversial on the Berkeley campus. Concerns arose due to the potential detrimental influence of companies on faculty research independence, the integrity of research results, and publishing restrictions. That controversy was exemplified by a backlash at Berkeley over the Novartis Corporation's $25 million sponsored research agreement with several professors in Berkeley's Department of Plant and Microbial Biology.[3]

Nonetheless, QB3 and CITRIS (both profiled later in this chapter) increased Berkeley's awareness of the untapped potential for corporations to fund campus research and commercialize the resulting innovations. That growing priority correspondingly increased the campus's legal and policy challenges. This led in 2004 to the formation of Berkeley's Industry Alliances Office (IAO), a team focused on negotiating sponsored research agreements with corporations. To accelerate Berkeley's partnership opportunities with companies, the IAO and Berkeley's Of-

---

University of California," May 2006, https://.senate.universityofcalifornia .edu/_files/reports/AC.Futures.Rpt.0107.pdf.

2. In contrast, peer institutions such as MIT and Stanford already had popular industry affiliates programs and significant funding from corporations, especially relative to their research funding from federal and state agencies.

3. Rex Dalton, "Berkeley Dispute Festers over Biotech Deal," *Nature* 399, no. 5 (1999), www.nature.com/articles/19807.

fice of Technology Licensing were reorganized under the newly formed Office of Intellectual Property and Industry Research Alliances (profiled later in this chapter). The campus promoted the new office as a one-stop shop for companies to collaborate with Berkeley on research and the commercialization of the resulting innovations.

A year later, in 2005, Berkeley's first academic program focused on teaching entrepreneurial skills to STEM-oriented students was established as the Center for Entrepreneurship and Technology (profiled in this chapter) in the College of Engineering.[4] The integration of entrepreneurship education into the campus's curriculum was a harbinger for the next phase of Berkeley's I&E ecosystem journey.

■ ■ ■ ■ ■

## California Institutes for Science and Innovation

### Center for Information Technology Research in the Interest of Society and the Banatao Institute

In 2000 the California Governor's Office requested proposals for new institutes based on three-way partnerships between the state, California industry, and the University of California for cross-disciplinary research focused on large-scale problems where advances would spur economic growth.[5] That initiative initially resulted in three winning proposals: one centered at UCLA and including UC Santa Barbara (CNSI), another centered

4. In contrast, the first entrepreneurship course offered at MIT was in 1961, according to Jean-Jacques Degroof's *From the Basement to the Dome: How MIT's Unique Culture Created a Thriving Entrepreneurial Community* (Cambridge, MA: MIT Press, 2021).

5. California Institutes for Science and Innovation, https://regents.university ofcalifornia.edu/regmeet/july06/304attach1.pdf.

Sutardja Dai Hall, the UC Berkeley headquarters of the Center for Information Technology Research in the Interest of Society (Credit: Tim Griffith)

at UC San Diego and including UC Irvine (Calit2), and a third centered at UC San Francisco and including UC Berkeley (QB3).

However, Berkeley College of Engineering faculty, then led by dean Richard Newton, made a strong case for including an institute devoted to information technology and its impact on society.[6] That proposal led to the formation of the Center for Information Technology Research in the Interest of Society (CITRIS)

6. A. Richard Newton's biography, www2.eecs.berkeley.edu/Faculty/Home pages/newton.html; and Professor A. Richard Newton, https://people.eecs .berkeley.edu/~newton/Resume/.

based at UC Berkeley and including UC Santa Cruz and UC Davis. Years later, CITRIS was extended to UC Merced. CITRIS originally aimed to "shorten the pipeline between academia and industry." Industry relations were essential to the institute's research agenda and financial model.

In 2016, CITRIS expanded with the new Banatao Institute, which leverages the four-campus institute to develop solutions that benefit low-resource communities.[7] That includes, in particular, the development of sustainable systems to address intertwined issues of poverty and access to public resources such as clean air, water, energy, and robust cyber infrastructure.

In 2024, Academic Innovation Catalyst partnered with CITRIS and the Banatao Institute to launch the CITRIS Innovation Fellowship program and the AIC Awards.[8] The partnership focuses on faculty-developed research with promising commercial applications that address society's most pressing challenges. Recipients receive up to $200,000 over two years to commercialize their innovations, along with support from the CITRIS Foundry incubator (profiled in chapter 4) and AIC, a deep tech funding platform that catalyzes academic innovations for positive social impact. CITRIS research themes have evolved over the years. As of 2025, they include climate, energy, and sustainability; health and health-care services; robotics, AI, and automation; democracy, policy, and civic engagement; and, more recently, aviation.

7. The Banatao Institute was made possible by philanthropic funding from Dado and Maria Banatao.

8. The CITRIS Innovation Fellowship program and the AIC Awards were made possible by philanthropic funding from UC Berkeley School of Law alumni Matt Sonsini and Lisa Sobrato Sonsini.

### *California Institute for Quantitative Biosciences*

Among the four California Institutes for Science and Innovation established in 2000, the California Institute for Quantitative Biosciences (QB3) was the earliest to focus on technology commercialization through startup companies. Also unique among the four institutes, QB3's entrepreneurial programs were available to founders unaffiliated with the University of California.

qb3

QB3's domain is "quantitative biosciences," a multidisciplinary area that encompasses the study of biology using techniques and technology derived from chemistry, physics, and computer science. QB3 is based at UC Berkeley, UC San Francisco (UCSF), and UC Santa Cruz.

Under eighteen years of leadership by executive director Regis Kelly, QB3 established itself as a preeminent organization fostering entrepreneurship for the public good.[9] QB3's track record of launching innovative endeavors includes the following:

- In 2007 a fully renovated Stanley Hall opened on the Berkeley campus to serve as an interdisciplinary research and teaching hub. The home of QB3 at UC Berkeley, it includes faculty laboratories, core research facilities, classrooms, and auditoriums.

- In 2009, Mission Bay Capital (MBC) launched its first seed-stage venture capital fund, which invests in biotech companies that emerge from University of California campuses.

- In 2010 the Master of Translational Medicine degree was established, bridging the UC Berkeley and UCSF campuses.

*(continued on page 37)*

9. Regis "Reg" B. Kelly was the executive director of QB3 from 2004 to 2022. Prior to that role, Kelly was a neuroscientist and executive vice chancellor at UC San Francisco.

# We Care Solar: The Power to Save Lives

Thousands of maternal health-care providers struggle to administer life-saving care in health centers that lack electricity. Like UC Berkeley School of Public Health alumnae Dr. Laura Stachel, those caregivers were trained to partake in one of the most meaningful experiences of human life—childbirth. And like Stachel, those caregivers are all too familiar with the rapidity with which the journey of childbirth can transform into one of the most frightening, and sometimes deadly, traumas. But unlike Stachel, they must try to save lives while lacking an essential requirement for health care: light. Stachel leveraged Berkeley's I&E ecosystem to address that problem and change the plight of those caregivers, moms, and newborns.

Stachel became a physician in 1985 at UC San Francisco, specializing in obstetrics and gynecology to support women at critical periods of their lives. Sadly, her medical career was cut

We Care Solar's founding couple, Laura Stachel and Hal Aronson

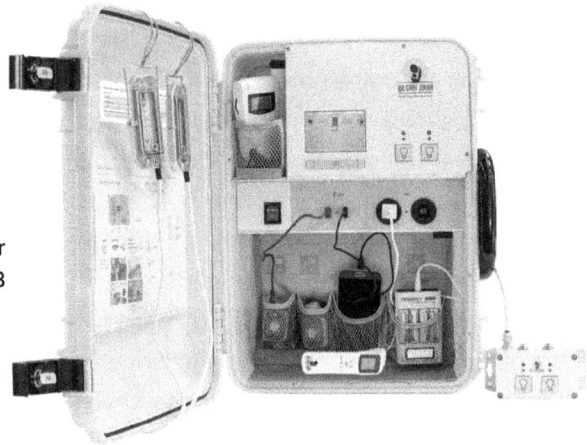

We Care Solar
Suitcase version 3

short by a degenerative spine disease that prevented her from delivering babies and performing surgery.

Seeking a new way to improve maternal health, Stachel enrolled in Berkeley's School of Public Health in 2004. There, she learned that half a million women—mainly in Africa and Asia—died each year from pregnancy complications. Most deaths could be prevented with timely, appropriate medical care.

In 2007 a chance encounter on the Berkeley campus with medical anthropologist Daniel Perlman informed Stachel about Berkeley's collaborative research program on maternal mortality with a Nigerian university, sponsored by Berkeley's Bixby Center for Population, Health and Sustainability. Perlman was looking for a graduate student to conduct ethnographic research in Nigerian hospitals, and Stachel, with her background in obstetrics, was an ideal candidate.

In 2008 Stachel traveled to Nigeria, where she was shocked by the grim conditions in a large state hospital. But even more striking were the frequent power outages that plunged the hospital into darkness. Stachel watched helplessly as caregivers struggled to treat critically ill pregnant women with only the dim glow of candlelight or kerosene lanterns.

Determined to help, Stachel described the desperate hospital conditions in emails to her husband, Hal Aronson, a solar energy educator. Upon Stachel's return to Berkeley, Aronson sketched a design for stand-alone solar electric systems for the hospital that could power medical lights, walkie-talkies, surgical suction, and a blood bank refrigerator.

WE CARE SOLAR

The opportunity to help was compelling, but the couple needed funds. Stachel learned about Berkeley's Big Ideas competition (profiled later in this chapter) and its $12,500 grand prize for technology offering a societal benefit. With only eleven days to the deadline, Stachel teamed up with two other Berkeley graduate students, Melissa Ho and Christian Casillas, to submit a proposal. When their project only earned an honorable mention and a $1,000 prize, Stachel was heartbroken but undeterred. That evening, she received a call from Tom Kalil, founder of Big Ideas in 2005 and a special advisor to Berkeley's chancellor. Kalil had attended that day's Big Ideas event. "You should have won," he told Stachel. "How much do you need?" Stachel requested $25,000, and within three weeks Kalil had found the funding through Berkeley's Blum Center for Developing Economies, thus launching the project that would evolve into the nonprofit We Care Solar.

Aronson's plan was to design an off-grid solar system for the hospital and hire a Nigerian company to do the installation. Stachel first wanted something tangible to show the hospital staff—something small enough to fit in her suitcase and avoid scrutiny by Nigerian customs officials. So Aronson packed Stachel's suitcase with a demonstration kit that included compact solar panels, a rechargeable battery, a control board as well as lights, headlamps, and walkie-talkies. The hospital staff loved the demonstration kit and approved plans for a hospital solar installation. But before Stachel departed the hospital, an operating room technician told her, "You must leave your suitcase here. It will help us save lives now."

Six months later Stachel returned to the hospital to oversee the solar installation. Maternal deaths dropped by 70 percent the next year. When nearby clinics asked for assistance from the "solar doctor," Stachel realized the utility of Aronson's portable solar kit. She brought prototype "Solar Suitcases" to health facilities on each of her return trips, refining the design based on user feedback over the next two years. Word spread, and soon requests for We Care Solar Suitcases came from around the world. Supported by donations, the couple turned their Berkeley home into a Solar Suitcase assembly and shipping plant. Unpaid volunteers helped Stachel and Aronson build the suitcases and courier them to health workers in remote destinations: midwives in Burma, clinics in Tibet, doctors in Tanzania, and medical relief workers in Haiti after the devastating 2010 earthquake.

In order to scale, Stachel and Aronson formalized their operation, leveraging the fiscal sponsorship of a UC Berkeley nonprofit engineering group before incorporating as a nonprofit. They enlisted the support of students, including Berkeley MBA Abhay Nihalani, to enter and win competitions such as Berkeley's Global Social Benefit Competition and the Chancellor's Award for Civic Engagement. The MacArthur Foundation and Berkeley's Blum Center for Developing Economies provided critical support for expansion.

Stachel learned that nonprofits have many of the same challenges as commercial startups. She had to build a team with expertise in operations, finance, manufacturing, and program management in order to tackle fundamental questions: How do we scale while effectively serving our beneficiaries/customers? How do we communicate our mission and measure our impact in compelling ways to attract investors and donors? How do we navigate international regulatory and policy changes?

We Care Solar has since grown into a global leader in maternal health and solar electrification, leading national Light Every Birth initiatives in multiple African countries. As of 2025, the award-winning nonprofit has equipped more than ten thousand health facilities with Solar Suitcases, ensuring sustainable light and power in some of the world's most remote and underresourced health clinics and supporting safe childbirth for more than eighteen million mothers and newborns. ▪

*(continued from page 32)*

- In 2010 the QB3 Garage@Berkeley opened in Stanley Hall, featuring 800 square feet of wet laboratory space. The incubator was the launching point for such startups as Zephyrus Biosciences (profiled in chapter 3) and GenEdit, cofounded in 2016 by Berkeley professor Niren Murthy and Berkeley PhDs Kunwoo Lee and Hyo Min Park.

- In 2012 the UCSF Rosenman Institute was formed. Initially focused on supporting medical device entrepreneurs, it later broadened to support all health tech.

- In 2013 QB3 launched QB3@953, a lab incubator space for biotech startups near the UCSF Mission Bay campus. QB3@953 eventually rebranded as MBC Biolabs, an organization not affiliated with the University of California.

- In 2017 the venture capital firm MedTech Venture Partners was incorporated as an early-stage investor in med tech startups and affiliated with the UCSF Rosenman Institute.

- In 2021 the Bakar BioEnginuity Hub and Bakar Labs opened Berkeley's flagship lab incubator facility for biotech startups (profiled in chapter 5).

Stanley Hall, the UC Berkeley headquarters for the California Institute for Quantitative Biosciences (QB3)

Following Kelly's retirement in 2022, QB3's directorship transitioned to Berkeley chemical and biomolecular engineering professor David Schaffer (whose startup 4D Molecular Therapeutics is profiled in chapter 4). Schaffer has focused on expanding QB3's incubator/accelerator programs, including a new 100,000-square-foot biotechnology startup company incubator at UCSF and a new 146,000-square-foot energy and materials technology incubator at Berkeley (profiled in chapter 6), as well as new programs that integrate applied academic research and entrepreneurship support across QB3's three UC campuses.

As of 2025, QB3 has continued to leverage invaluable support and funding from the State of California and the UC Office of the

President to incubate and accelerate over three hundred companies that have raised more than $16 billion and created over seventeen thousand jobs. This public-private partnership continues to grow and amplify the positive effects of UC's education and research missions on California's economy and the planet.

## Licensing Intellectual Property to Startups

University I&E excellence is not achievable without an approach to managing and licensing university intellectual property (IP) tailored for startups, particularly startups that originate or spin out from a university's labs. This principle is due to the fact that the ownership and licensing of university IP is the legal, financial, and strategic connection between the innovations that result from university research and the commercialization of those innovations by either startup companies or established corporations. Despite that fundamental importance to I&E excellence, licensing university IP to startups instead of established corporations initially bucked conventional wisdom and took time to gain momentum at UC Berkeley (and other universities). This section describes that transition and impact.

For startups trying to commercialize technology developed at universities, exclusive commercial licenses to corresponding patents and software are often crucial to success. Startups can use exclusive patent rights as a barrier to competitors, particularly established companies with more resources and momentum than startups. Similarly, exclusive rights to software source code can give startups time-to-market leads over competitors. The competitive advantages derived from licensed IP bolster startups' revenue potential, which in turn helps startups obtain the venture capital investments required to commercialize products based on the licensed intellectual property.

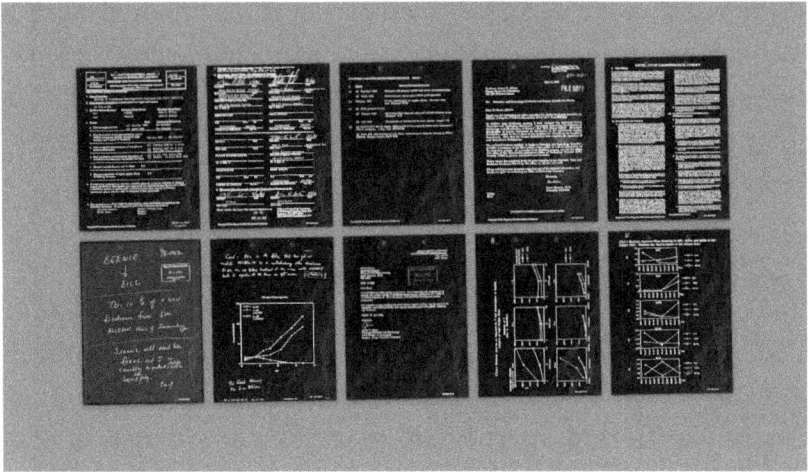

NFT based on the UC Berkeley Invention Disclosure for Nobel Prize–winning Cancer Immunotherapy Technology (COPYRIGHT: FIATLUXDAO)

The Bayh-Dole Act, federal law enacted in 1980, enables universities to own, patent, and license inventions developed under federally funded research programs. At Berkeley the Office of Technology Licensing (OTL) was formed in 1990 to manage the IP developed on the campus, including patenting and licensing. As of 2025, the OTL has licensed IP to more than three hundred startups that have raised over $30 billion in funding.[10] Many of the startups have spearheaded new markets and industries and, in so doing, have scaled into successful large corporations.

However, the Berkeley OTL's tailored approach to startups didn't gain momentum until after 2004 with the formation of the Industry Alliances Office (IAO) and the reorganization of the OTL and IAO under the newly formed Office of Intellectual

10. That amount doesn't include billions of dollars in funding to Berkeley spinouts that are based on open-source software developed at Berkeley.

Property and Industry Research Alliances (IPIRA). Campus leadership implemented that organizational structure to establish a one-stop shop for companies to easily fund campus researchers as well as license and commercialize the innovations resulting from campus research. This one-stop shop positioning codified the realization that multiple pathways exist for licensing and commercializing university IP. Correspondingly, there are multiple approaches to managing and licensing intellectual property in ways that are optimized for the different pathways.[11] These include the following three pathways:

1. The "push" pathway was Berkeley's conventional approach that resulted from the OTL marketing specific Berkeley IP to targeted companies based on OTL research that indicated those companies would be a good fit for commercializing and licensing the IP.

2. The new "pull" pathway resulted from the growing number of companies that sponsored collaborative research in Berkeley labs and then pulled the resulting IP out of the labs so that the companies could license and commercialize the IP.

3. A third pathway had become increasingly common in which one or more researchers in a Berkeley lab spun out a startup to license and commercialize the IP that those researchers had developed in the lab.

The emerging opportunity to license intellectual property to startups wasn't obvious. At that time the conventional wisdom was that successfully commercializing university IP required

(continued on page 44)

11. Carol Mimura, the first and longtime executive director of the Office of Intellectual Property and Industry Research Alliances, coined the "push" and "pull" pathways for university technology transfer to industry.

# Amyris Biotechnologies: Pioneering the Synthetic Biology Industry

Synthetic biology is the use of genetic engineering and other molecular biology breakthroughs to create microbial chemical factories that produce products that can have novel capabilities, low costs, and reduced environmental impact.[a] The field has huge potential to improve the world.

In the early 2000s, Jay Keasling, a UC Berkeley professor of chemical and biomolecular engineering, was a leading researcher in the emerging field of synthetic biology. Keasling's Berkeley lab had developed one of the field's first triumphs: engineering yeast to produce organic compounds called isoprenoids. Isoprenoids have many uses, including in flavorings, fragrances, and solvents. But Keasling wanted to focus the technology on much-needed pharmaceuticals, especially for the developing world. That led Keasling and his lab team to synthesize artemisinin, a compound that is the most effective cure for malaria. At that time malaria was killing millions of people, primarily children in Africa and Asia. Back then, the cost of artemisinin therapy was beyond the reach of millions of people. But Berkeley's synthetic artemisinin could change that by reducing the cost of the drug tenfold.

Keasling and Carol Mimura in Berkeley's Office of Technology Licensing considered licensing the artemisinin synthesis patent rights to a big pharmaceutical company, but as Keasling stated, "those companies weren't the best licensees because they lacked the yeast engineering knowledge and the sustained business focus. Instead, a startup whose existence depended on the successful scale-up of artemisinin would be the ideal licensee." So in 2003, Keasling along with four members of his lab—Jack Newman, Neil Renninger, Kinkead Reiling, and Vincent Martin—cofounded Amyris Biotechnologies.

The social impact of making a malaria cure widely accessible attracted the attention of the Bill & Melinda Gates Foundation. In 2004 the foundation awarded a $43 million grant to a partnership between Amyris, Keasling's Berkeley lab, and One-World Health—the first nonprofit pharmaceutical company in the United States. Under the unique public-private institution partnership, the Berkeley lab perfected the microbial factory for producing artemisinin; Amyris adapted the yeast for industrial production and engineered the fermentation process for industrial scale-up; and OneWorld Health developed the drug regime and led its regulatory approval.

In a 2024 interview Keasling applauded Berkeley "for having the flexibility and skills to negotiate an award-winning complex royalty-free patent license agreement with the Gates Foundation. The partnership was a model for attacking neglected diseases in the developing world."[b] Keasling added, "That project

UC Berkeley professor Jay Keasling (CREDIT: ROY KALTSCHMIDT/LBNL)

was a dream come true: interesting science, high technology, rapid transition from the lab bench to the bedside, and most importantly, meeting a critical need."

With its Gates Foundation grant and antimalarial partnership, Amyris's prominence in the exciting field of synthetic biology skyrocketed. That attracted the attention of leading venture capital firms. In 2005, Kleiner Perkins and Khosla Ventures led Amyris's $20 million Series A funding. That was an exciting time for the company. "Amyris attracted amazing people who were dedicated to the company's mission," Keasling said. "The spirit in the company was incredible."

Amyris's antimalarial mission was indeed admirable, but the company hadn't identified a large commercial opportunity for its technology until 2006. At that time the price of oil rose sharply, surpassing $100 per barrel for the first time since the early 1980s. The price rise was caused in part by disruptions in the supply of oil. That raised interest in alternatives to petroleum-based fuels, especially alternatives with less environmental impact. Amyris's technology could be used to produce farnesene, a renewable hydrocarbon that could be used to make biodiesel fuel. The company could make it possible for producers to blend renewable hydrocarbons produced from sustainable biomass and organic waste into fuel. Renewable

substantial R&D and marketing resources that only a large company could garner. However, increasing success from licensing to startups, especially startups spun out of Berkeley's labs, revealed that unlike established corporations, startup teams often have the unique know-how and necessary focus to best commercialize a particular innovation. Eventually startups can obtain the resources to scale their commercial success via venture diesel based on Amyris technology could deliver energy density, engine performance, and storage properties comparable to the best petroleum-based diesel as well as improved lubricity and superior cold-weather performance.

That biofuel potential propelled Amyris through a series of funding rounds that culminated in 2010 with the company's initial public offering that raised $85 million and valued Amyris at nearly $700 million.

As of 2025, Keasling has cofounded two additional companies, LS9 and Lygos, and he's proud of his students who have gone on to found over a dozen companies (as well as establish careers in academia and industry). Of Keasling's four Amyris cofounders, Renninger went on to found Ripple Foods and Ample Carbon, Reiling founded Bonneville Labs, and Newman continued fighting malaria by founding Zagaya. In reflecting on his legacy of students, innovations, and startups, Keasling remarked, "Berkeley is a special place." •

a. The source for much of the content in this section is Robert Sanders, "$43 Million Grant from Gates Foundation Brings Together Unique Collaboration for Antimarial Drug," *UC Berkeley News*, December 13, 2004, https://newsarchive.berkeley.edu/news/media/re

b. UC Berkeley's intellectual property licensing office won the US Patent Office's inaugural Patents for Humanity Award for architecting a path to create low-cost malaria treatments for the world's poor. leases/2004/12/13_gates.shtml.

capital funding and partnering with or being acquired by large companies.

Successfully licensing IP to startups is different from successfully licensing to established corporations. Compared to established corporations, startups contend with more business risks and resource constraints, especially capital. To address those differences, the OTL developed patenting and licensing practices optimized for startups, making it easier and faster for startups to license the university's IP.

The Berkeley OTL's startup-optimized IP mindset is highlighted on its webpage ipira.berkeley.edu/licensing-practices -support-startups, and its startup-optimized IP practices are summarized below:

1. **Paying for or subsidizing initial patent costs.** This practice anticipates that many startup licensees will eventually reimburse the university for those initial patenting payments when the startups obtain capital infusions or sales income.

2. **Offering simple license option agreements.** As an alternative first step to a startup securing exclusive rights, this simple option helps startups manage a license's risks and financial commitments.

3. **Agreeing to flexible license financial terms.** This practice includes modifying license terms and extending performance milestone timelines if a startup pivots its business plan or is delayed in achieving its goals.

4. **Accepting a startup's stock equity as an offset to cash payments for licensing.** Since 1996, Berkeley has accepted startup equity instead of an all-cash fee in IP licenses. That practice has helped hundreds of startups by lowering the financial barrier to obtaining a license, and it enables Berkeley to participate in the potential upside of a startup's business success. In 2020, Berkeley started using SAFE agreements, which simplified the approach of accepting stock equity in startups.

5. **Managing (not prohibiting) faculty involvement in the licensing process.** Allowing faculty who are inventors in

IP developed in their lab to have a role in licensing that IP can result in conflicts of interest that are detrimental to the university, other co-inventors, and societal impact. However, instead of prohibiting faculty inventors from any involvement in licensing, the OTL allows some participation in the licensing strategy and manages the extent of any detrimental conflict of interest.

6. **Flexibility to open-source software.** Under the University of California Intellectual Property Policy, software developed by university researchers should be disclosed to the university so that university staff responsible for managing and licensing software copyrights can determine how to best manage the copyrights for societal impact. However, the Berkeley OTL allows software authors to decide whether to make their software available under a free open-source license.

## Where Engineers Discover Their Inner Entrepreneur: Sutardja Center for Entrepreneurship and Technology

As student interest in founding startups gained momentum during the internet boom of the late 1990s, a common question in academia was, can entrepreneurship be taught? And if yes, how is teaching entrepreneurship different from teaching business management, especially for technology-intensive founders? Leaders in UC Berkeley's College of Engineering who were involved in technology startups recognized the opportunity to provide entrepreneurship courses and programs to engineering

students. In 2005 that recognition led to the launch of the Sutardja Center for Entrepreneurship and Technology (SCET).[12]

### 2005–2012: The Journey Begins

At its onset, SCET had the dual mission of positioning Berkeley engineering as a global leader in innovation and entrepreneurship as well as enabling engineering students to learn and
apply entrepreneurship skills. At that time most university entrepreneurship programs were housed in business schools with
a focus on MBA students. SCET, housed in Berkeley's College
of Engineering, broadened the reach of entrepreneurship education to address the challenges that technology students and
faculty experience in creating technology ventures. Unlike MBA
students, most engineering students have had little exposure to
markets and limited access to networks of business advisors and
investors. SCET filled that gap at Berkeley, providing engineering students with practical training and introductions to industry leaders and investors.

SCET is known for its homegrown curriculum called the
Berkeley Method of Entrepreneurship (BMoE). Created by the
center's founding director Ikhlaq Sidhu and chief learning officer Ken Singer, the BMoE is a sociocultural approach to entrepreneurship education. Its premise is that one becomes an
entrepreneur through developing not only the skills but also
the mindset of an innovator. This requires more than acquiring
domain-specific knowledge. It also requires cultivating behaviors that lead to entrepreneurial success. Those behaviors include resilience, productive conflict, multidisciplinary collabo-

---

12. SCET was made possible by philanthropic funding from UC Berkeley
alumni and entrepreneurs Pantas and Ting Sutardja.

ration, trust-building, embracing failure as part of the learning process, and effectively communicating ideas. Through experiential learning and a game-based environment, the BMoE enables students to internalize and practice these entrepreneurial behaviors, preparing them to tackle real-world challenges.

## 2012–2024: Expansion to Technology Entrepreneurship for All

Innovation is inherently an interdisciplinary endeavor. Engineers should not go it alone. That's why SCET began promoting its classes and programs to nonengineers in 2012, to bring aspiring innovators from all disciplines into the classroom to collaborate with engineering students. That expanded mission required investments in people and facilities. SCET became an endowed center in 2015 with the support of Berkeley alumni who shared the belief that entrepreneurship education should be available to all. This led to the development of cutting-edge course topics such as alternative meat and the first applied blockchain and AI entrepreneurship courses at Berkeley. It also spawned an international program to bring ambitious students and researchers from around the world to collaborate with the Berkeley community, expanding their networks and access to markets. As of 2025, SCET works with dozens of universities in more than fifteen countries, many in developing regions.

Central to SCET's mission to empower innovators is to positively change the world. The center challenges students to focus on problems that matter to them and the global community. SCET develops course topics and recruits industry instructors who embody this commitment to the greater good. An example of this programming is SCET's popular Challenge Lab courses (and annual Collider Cup demo day), where interdisciplinary

*(continued on page 52)*

## SuitX: From Sitting in a Wheelchair to Walking in an Exoskeleton

Robotic-assisted exoskeletons for humans have been commonly depicted as technology for battle and wars. However, that's not what has inspired Homayoon Kazerooni, UC Berkeley professor of mechanical engineering, as well as his students and startup colleagues to pioneer the development and commercialization of wearable exoskeletons. They've been driven by the vision of exoskeletons helping millions of people with mobility limitations due to, for example, cerebral palsy, multiple sclerosis, strokes, and spinal injuries.

Kazerooni's research on exoskeletons began in the early 1990s. Around 2000 his work gained momentum with a US government–funded project aimed at developing a device to assist individuals in carrying heavy loads over extended periods. At that time Kazerooni realized the potential use of exoskeletons in the medical field, particularly as an alternative to wheelchairs.

To pursue that potential, Kazerooni, along with one of his students, Nathan Harding, cofounded Ekso Bionics (originally known as Berkeley ExoWorks) in 2005. The startup licensed the core technology from Berkeley, and to help fund its development of exoskeletons for health care, Ekso sublicensed its technology to Lockheed Martin Corporation to develop exoskeletons that enable military personnel to carry heavy equipment over long distances. The startup subsequently raised a Series A round of funding in 2010, and it became a publicly traded company in 2014. As of 2025, Ekso is a leader in advanced robotics designed to enhance, amplify, and restore human function.

While Ekso was pursuing its exoskeleton product strategy, Kazerooni envisioned a broader purpose for the technology beyond Ekso's plans. He aimed to drive down the costs of exoskeletons, making them an affordable and accessible alternative to wheelchairs. That commitment to accessibility also inspired Kazerooni to develop exoskeletons tailored for workers, helping to reduce the risk of workplace musculoskeletal injuries.[a] To pursue his broader vision, Kazerooni founded SuitX (originally known as US Bionics) in 2011. Four of his PhD students became early key members of the SuitX team: Michael McKinley, Wayne Tung, Minerva Pillai, and Logan Van Engelhoven.

Later that year an exoskeleton co-developed by SuitX and Kazerooni's lab enabled Berkeley senior Austin Whitney, a paraplegic, to stand and walk across the commencement stage at graduation; the crowd of fifteen thousand in Edwards Stadium stood up with him—and roared.[b] Whitney, who was paralyzed in a 2007 car accident, said: "Ask anybody in a wheelchair; ask what it would mean to once again stand and shake someone's hand while facing them at eye level. It will be surreal, like a dream."[c]

UC Berkeley professor Homayoon Kazerooni with exoskeleton system
(SOURCE: IEEE SPECTRUM 2016 APRIL 25)

That heartwarming demonstration of the technology was followed by two global awards. In 2014 the exoskeleton technology developed in Kazerooni's Berkeley lab was honored by the AUTM Better World Project, recognizing university research that improves the world. Then in 2016, SuitX received a $1 million prize as the winner of the Robotics for Good competition based on the company's pediatric medical exoskeleton. The prize-winning exoskeleton had been optimized to help children affected by neurological conditions like cerebral palsy and spina bifida, for whom walking is difficult or impossible. The goal was to develop exoskeletons that promote childrens' walking skills during the narrow timeframe when they easily acquire locomotion skills. "By aiming at neurologically disabled children," Kazerooni said, "we can make the difference between children spending their lives in a wheelchair or actually standing and walking."

Between 2013 and 2019, SuitX received three grants from the US government, totaling about $1.2 million. In 2021, SuitX was acquired by Ottobock, a global leader in prosthetics,

teams of students work together to address complex, real-world problems. With dynamic Challenge Lab topics such as the future of work, alternative meats, and sports tech, many SCET alumni have gone on to launch companies that have significantly impacted industries ranging from food tech to mental health.

As of 2025, the Sutardja Center for Entrepreneurship and Technology has become a cornerstone of Berkeley's I&E ecosystem. The center engages about two thousand students annually through courses, a lecture series, and summer boot camps.

orthotics, and exoskeletons. The acquisition aimed to combine expertise and product lines to advance the exoskeleton market and promote worldwide adoption of exoskeleton technologies. By the time of the acquisition, SuitX had licensed nearly a hundred issued and pending patents from Berkeley—among the most patent rights for any Berkeley licensee.

As a legend in the exoskeleton field, and in recognition for his pioneering development of exoskeleton technology, in 2024, Kazerooni was named a Fellow of the National Academy of Inventors—the highest professional distinction awarded to inventors. ▪

a. In 2016 the US Department of Labor ranked back and knee injuries as the most common injuries among workers, leading to about $16 billion annually in workers' compensation.

b. Sarah Yang, "Paraplegic Student Stands Tall and Walks at Commencement," *UC Berkeley News*, May 14, 2002, https://news.berkeley.edu/2011/05/14/paraplegic-student-stands-walks-at-graduation/.

c. Sarah Yang, "Engineers to Help Paragplegic Student to Walk at Graduation," *UC Berkeley News*, May 12, 2011, https://news.berkeley.edu/2011/05/12/paraplegic-student-exoskeleton-graduation walk/.

## 2025 and Beyond

SCET's impact has continued growing as it approaches its twentieth anniversary. With the 2025 move to the purpose-built collaborative space in Berkeley's new Engineering Center, SCET is in the heart of the campus, making it more visible to all Berkeley students, faculty, and industry partners. In this new era SCET continues to foster a culture of innovation and entrepreneurship by creating new opportunities for students to create lasting, positive change in an increasingly complex world.

UC Berkeley Blum Center for Developing Economies, the headquarters of the Big
Ideas program

## Student-Led Social Ventures: Big Ideas Contest

The annual Big Ideas pre-accelerator program at UC Berkeley
defines a big idea as a solution to a pressing social issue. These
big ideas are often inspired by life's small moments, like watching a single-use plastic container wash up on a beach or holding
a loved one's hand at bedside as they battle a fatal disease.

The Berkeley campus has been at the forefront of big ideas,
and Berkeley faculty benefit from the support of academic departments and research grants to pursue their big ideas. However, Berkeley students typically need to be more resourceful
and scrappy to garner support for developing their big ideas.

Launched in 2005 by Tom Kalil, then special assistant to the
Berkeley chancellor, the Big Ideas program was Berkeley's first
campus-wide effort to encourage and support student-led social

innovation.[13] Rather than narrow the opportunity to a specific college or require students to be on a strictly entrepreneurial course track, the Big Ideas program is open to all undergraduate and graduate students. As of 2025, participants have hailed from more than seventy-five majors, and half of all participants are women.

Big Ideas recognizes that people-focused solutions benefit from diverse perspectives. Often, students who have lived the problems they are trying to solve are best positioned to devise a solution. Participants use their unique backgrounds in their pitches. For example, one student drew on her Indigenous knowledge to develop Nopa, a method of concentrating a plant extract

for application as a fully biodegradable adhesive alternative to petroleum-based price look-up (PLU) stickers on produce.

The annual Big Ideas interdisciplinary program provides the foundation to turn a personal experience into a functional solution with a global impact. The process provides skills development, mentorship, funding, and recognition to a wide range of student-led social ventures.

With the support of the Big Ideas program, one student's experience of losing her grandmother to chronic obstructive

13. The launch of Big Ideas was made possible by philanthropic funding from the Omidyar Network. In 2010 the Big Ideas program's expansion was made possible by philanthropic funding from UC Berkeley alumnus and entrepreneur Andrew Rudd and his wife, Virginia.

pulmonary disease inspired her to develop Sylvee, an AI-enabled device that monitors pulmonary volumes, trapped air, respiratory rates, and breathing sounds to deliver actionable insights on how to optimize day-to-day respiratory health. In another example, after participating in Big Ideas, a student in Berkeley's School of Public Health founded We Care Solar (profiled in this chapter). This nonprofit organization has developed and equipped more than ten thousand health facilities with a portable, off-grid solar-powered system, ensuring sustainable light and power in some of the world's most remote and under-resourced health clinics.

As of 2025, Big Ideas has supported more than thirty-five hundred projects, representing some ten thousand students. It has awarded approximately $3 million in seed funding to 450 early-stage ventures that have raised over $1.2 billion to date in additional funding from investors, foundations, philanthropists, and government agencies.

# THREE

# Aligning Campus Leaders and Cultivating Local Partners

Logic will get you from A to B.
Imagination will take you everywhere.

→■ ALBERT EINSTEIN

## Berkeley I&E, 2007–2012

Pioneering UC Berkeley I&E activities between 2007 and 2012 made those five years pivotal in the trajectory of the campus's ecosystem surge. These critical activities expanded enthusiasm for entrepreneurship from scattered faculty and students to the campus's leadership, notably the chancellor, vice chancellor for research, and the deans of the College of Engineering and School of Business. Entrepreneurship enthusiasm also expanded to the leadership of the Lawrence Berkeley National Lab (LBNL) and the City of Berkeley municipal government.[1] During these years the potential for Berkeley I&E to help solve the world's pressing problems, such as climate change, overshadowed campus community resistance to industry encroachment in campus re-

---

1. Lawrence Berkeley National Lab is a US Department of Energy (DOE) laboratory located in Berkeley adjacent to the UC Berkeley campus. LBNL conducts unclassified scientific research and is managed by the University of California for the DOE Office of Science.

search. By 2012, I&E at Berkeley had become not only accepted but an emerging strategic imperative for the campus.

Berkeley's embrace of research collaborations with and funding from industry reached another milestone in February 2007 with the announcement that the global energy corporation BP had selected the campus to lead a $500 million energy research consortium in partnership with LBNL and the University of Illinois. As part of the BP partnership, Berkeley established the Energy Biosciences Institute in a new building on the campus that was partly funded by BP. Some space in that building was allocated to BP scientists based on the expectation that their colocation with the university would accelerate the commercial outcomes of the research consortium.

Other corporations also established R&D outposts within walking distance of Berkeley's campus, including Amazon, Intel, Siemens, Yahoo, and Starkey Labs (a leading hearing aid corporation).[2] That proximity of corporate R&D led to the realization of the enhanced benefits of Berkeley's collaborations with companies that have R&D operations near the campus. These benefits include more opportunities for serendipitous in-person interactions as well as internships for students, jobs for graduates, and part-time consulting roles for faculty. Additional benefits include regional economic vitality that leads to improved local quality of life and public (along with government) support of the university.

That recognition and Berkeley's huge new energy biosciences collaboration spurred the launch in December 2007 of the

2. In addition to those corporate R&D outposts, two R&D organizations brought visiting engineers from leading technology companies within walking distance of the Berkeley campus: the Berkeley Wireless Research Center and the International Computer Science Institute.

East Bay Green Corridor (EBGC). The EBGC was a partnership between UC Berkeley, the Lawrence Berkeley National Lab, and four East Bay cities: Berkeley, Emeryville, Oakland, and Richmond. In 2009 the EBGC expanded to thirteen East Bay cities. The partnership's goals were to attract and retain green businesses, promote cleantech research and technology transfer, strengthen green workforce development programs, and coordinate a regional effort to secure more federal cleantech funding.[3]

The EBGC was the campus's first I&E initiative focused on regional economic development and the first I&E activity in partnership with LBNL (located on the hillside along the eastern edge of the university campus). More important, the EBGC was Berkeley's first I&E activity in which a chancellor played a founding role.[4] This development spotlighted that the campus leadership was not only supporting I&E, it was now championing it.

Berkeley's new Energy Biosciences Institute and the East Bay Green Corridor fueled enthusiasm for cleantech at the campus and national lab. That booming interest led to the launch of a student-run group called the Berkeley Energy Resources Collaborative. Soon after its founding, that student group teamed up with LBNL to pilot an extracurricular project that in 2008 evolved into a business school course called Cleantech to Market (profiled later in this chapter). This was the campus's first of several lab-to-market courses in which multidisciplinary teams

*(continued on page 63)*

---

3. Cathy Cockrell, "East Bay Announces Its 'Green Corridor' Ambitions," *UC Berkeley News*, December 4, 2007, https://newsarchive.berkeley.edu/news/media/releases/2007/12/04_green.shtml.

4. Robert Birgeneau was the UC Berkeley chancellor and Steven Chu was the Lawrence Berkeley National Lab director who both played leadership roles in founding the EBGC.

# Caribou Biosciences:
# Spinning Out a Nobel Prize–Winning Discovery

UC Berkeley professor Jennifer Doudna, with Emmanuelle Charpentier, won the 2020 Nobel Prize in Chemistry for the discovery of CRISPR-Cas9 genome editing based on research that they published in 2012. A year earlier, Doudna had launched her first startup company, Caribou Biosciences, with one of her graduate students, Rachel Haurwitz, as CEO.

Prior to cofounding Caribou, Doudna had not thought much about commercializing technology developed in her lab, but she liked the idea of being part of a company that could have an impact on people's health.[a] Likewise, Haurwitz was intrigued with the biotech industry. Although she was a skilled researcher, Haurwitz didn't want academic research to be her career. So while completing her PhD, she took courses at Berkeley's School of Business. By the time she was in her final year of research in Doudna's lab, Haurwitz had decided she wanted to run a biotech company.[b]

**UC Berkeley professor Jennifer Doudna** (UC BERKELEY PHOTO COURTESY OF CAILEY COTNER)

In 2011 the two scientists, along with Berkeley professor James Berger and postdoc Martin Jinek, cofounded Caribou. The startup benefitted from support from the California Institute for Quantitative Biosciences (QB3, profiled in chapter 2). QB3's "Startup in a Box" program (superseded by general entrepreneurship support on legal, banking, and mentoring) helped Doudna and Haurwitz incorporate the company and establish bank services. The startup's early focus was on RNA diagnostic tools based on CRISPR technology from Doudna's lab as well as CRISPR Cas9-mediated genome editing, both licensed from Berkeley.

Initially, the cofounders launched the company with investment from friends and family. Caribou then attracted investment interest primarily from corporate venture capital (rather than traditional institutional venture capital) who believed in the potential of genome editing.

In his book *The Code Breaker*, Walter Isaacson wrote that Haurwitz "had talents not often found in Silicon Valley entrepreneurs. With her steady personality, she was a naturally good manager. She was down to earth, unflappable, practical, and straightforward. There was no whiff of the combination of

Rachel Haurwitz, CEO and cofounder of Caribou Biosciences
(CREDIT: CARIBOU BIOSCIENCES)

ego and insecurity exuded by many startup CEOs. She did not exaggerate or overpromise. That offered many advantages, one of which was that people tended to underestimate her."

In 2013 a QB3 grant-writing workshop helped Caribou obtain $300,000 in funding from the US government's Small Business Innovation Research program. With that funding, Caribou launched operations in the QB3 Garage incubator lab (profiled in chapter 5) located in Berkeley's Stanley Hall. Caribou raised $11 million in Series A financing in 2015. The venture capital fund Mission Bay Capital, then affiliated with QB3, participated in that financing. That funding enabled the startup to expand to a larger lab and office space in the QB3 East Bay Innovation Center, located on the west side of Berkeley and operated in partnership with the real estate firm Wareham Development. Caribou raised $30 million in Series B financing in 2016, $115 million in Series C financing in early 2021, and in the summer of 2021 the company raised $350 million in its initial public offering that valued the company at nearly a billion dollars.

As of 2025, Caribou has more than 140 employees and is conducting clinical trials on off-the-shelf CAR-T cell therapies using next-generation CRISPR technology developed by the company. The two founders have stayed involved with QB3 and Berkeley. Haurwitz regularly participates in speaking events to inspire women entrepreneurs. Caribou became a corporate affiliate of Berkeley's Bakar Labs incubator (profiled in chapter 5), sponsoring its lab space, events, and programming for up-and-coming bioentrepreneurs. Doudna went on to found and lead the governance board of the Innovative Genomics Institute at Berkeley. ▪

a. Walter Isaacson, *The Code Breaker: Jennifer Doudna, Gene Editing, and the Future of the Human Race* (New York: Simon & Schuster, 2021), 114.

b. Isaacson, *Code Breaker*, 115.

of students craft commercialization plans for technologies developed at the campus or the national lab.

Three years after its launch, the East Bay Green Corridor disbanded (mainly due to the state government's termination of its funding for Regional Development Agencies). However, the EBGC had established interpersonal relationships between UC Berkeley and the City of Berkeley's Office of Economic Development. Those relationships led to the founding in 2009 of the Berkeley Startup Cluster (BSC), the campus's first hyperlocal (not regional) economic development collaboration with the Lawrence Berkeley National Lab, the Berkeley municipal government, the Berkeley Chamber of Commerce, the Downtown Berkeley Association as well as local R&D-intensive startups and established corporations.[5] The BSC (profiled in this chapter) aimed to get more innovations from the campus and national lab commercialized by companies based in Berkeley, instead of the then common pattern of companies commercializing Berkeley innovations about fifty miles south in the epicenter of Silicon Valley.

The Berkeley Startup Cluster's relationship-building with the local R&D-oriented private sector led to interpersonal relationships between BSC leadership and the leadership of Intel Corporation's satellite lab, located one block from the Berkeley campus (on the entire penthouse floor of 2150 Shattuck Avenue, the tallest building in downtown Berkeley at the time). In January 2011 a director of Intel's Berkeley lab informed BSC leadership

5. The Berkeley Startup Cluster was cofounded by Mike Alvarez Cohen from UC Berkeley; Michael Caplan, the head of the City of Berkeley Office of Economic Development; Julie Sinai, the chief of staff for Berkeley Mayor Tom Bates; John Caner, the head of the Downtown Berkeley Association; and Polly Armstrong, the head of the Berkeley Chamber of Commerce. Kirsten Kyria Macdonald succeeded Armstrong in 2015 as head of the Chamber and served on the BSC steering committee until 2021.

that due to corporate budget issues, Intel was closing several satellite research centers adjacent to universities, including this one near Berkeley (as well as those near other universities such as the University of Washington and Carnegie Mellon University).[6] That meeting inspired BSC leadership to champion converting the penthouse (with all the office furniture and equipment left behind and donated by Intel) into Berkeley's first startup accelerator office space and program.

One year later, with leadership oversight and financial support from the deans of the College of Engineering and the School of Business, along with the vice chancellor for research, the Berkeley SkyDeck startup accelerator (profiled later in this chapter and chapter 4) launched in 2012 and ushered in the next phase of Berkeley's I&E ecosystem growth.

■ ■ ■ ■ ■

## Paying It Forward: Berkeley Alumni

UC Berkeley's vast alumni network—some six hundred thousand strong as of 2025—has been instrumental to the campus's I&E ascendance. Berkeley graduates have distinguished themselves, particularly in the startup world. As of 2024, the campus leads all institutions in producing both overall undergraduate founders and female founders of venture-backed companies. This professional success, combined with an appreciation and pride in their alma mater, has inspired alumni to give back to the university.

Alumni contributions span the entire entrepreneurship spectrum, including as founders of startups based on Berkeley inno-

---

6. That January 2011 meeting was between Issy Kipnis, the associate director of Intel Labs Berkeley, and Mike Alvarez Cohen, a cofounder of the Berkeley Startup Cluster and also the director of innovation ecosystem development in UC Berkeley's Office of Intellectual Property and Industry Research Alliances.

vations, mentors to those founders, as well as early investors, advisors, and key employees in those startups. Many alumni teach or guest lecture campus courses related to entrepreneurship. That participation leverages the many alumni who work and live in the surrounding metro region. All the early-stage venture capital funds that share a percentage of their investment profits with Berkeley (profiled in chapter 4) have general partners or limited partners who are Berkeley graduates.

Over the past decade, UC Berkeley has engaged its alumni network to bolster campus innovation and entrepreneurship. A notable initiative is the Berkeley Founders' Pledge, launched in 2013, which invites alumni entrepreneurs who are company founders to make a nonbinding commitment to donate a portion of their proceeds or equity to the university upon achieving financial success. This program has garnered participation from over 540 alumni and faculty, many of whom have fulfilled their pledges following lucrative IPOs or acquisitions. The Berkeley Founders' Pledge exemplifies a pattern where alumni success fuels future innovation, resulting in over $85 million in philanthropy from signers of the Pledge. In 2019, this philanthropic momentum was further recognized when innovation and entrepreneurship was designated as a prioritized multidisciplinary track in Berkeley's $7.3 billion Light the Way capital campaign.

Berkeley graduates have become prolific financial supporters and expert participants in Berkeley I&E programs. Examples include (in chronological order of formation) the Lester Center for Entrepreneurship (profiled in chapter 1); the Sutardja Center for Entrepreneurship and Technology and the Banatao Institute (both profiled in chapter 2); the Bakar Fellows Program (profiled in chapter 3); Academic Innovation Catalyst (highlighted in chapters 2 and 3); the Berkeley SkyDeck advisor network (highlighted in chapter 4); two dual degree programs, the Management, Entrepreneurship, & Technology (MET) program and the Life Science, Business, and Entrepreneurship (LSBE) program (both profiled in chapter 4); the Bakar BioEnginuity Hub and the Life Sciences Entrepreneurship Center (both profiled in chapter 5); Project Tipping Point (highlighted in chapter 5); and the Bakar Labs for energy and materials (profiled in chapter 6).

Through their ongoing support, past generations of Berkeley alumni have created a virtuous cycle and culture of paying it forward to the next generation of campus entrepreneurs, creating a self-reinforcing mechanism for building I&E excellence.

## Creating a Talent Vortex: The Berkeley Startup Cluster

A key attribute that distinguishes world-class I&E ecosystems from mediocre ones is that the top environments have a super-critical mass of human talent across a range of expertise from science, engineering, and manufacturing to management, marketing, finance, and law. Through the annual cycles of matriculating and graduating students, a university can act as a vortex for creating a supercritical mass of talent, but only if the region near the university is attractive to (1) graduating alumni entrepreneurs locating and scaling their companies near the university, and (2) large R&D-intensive companies establishing a nearby presence. Accordingly, a university that wants to build a top-tier I&E ecosystem must have the cooperation of local government agencies as well as the private sector (such as real estate developers) to make the region inviting to those R&D-intensive entrepreneurs and established corporations.[7]

7. For more insight into the concept of vortex versus waypoint university campuses, see Mike Cohen, "Vortex Versus Waypoint Campuses: How

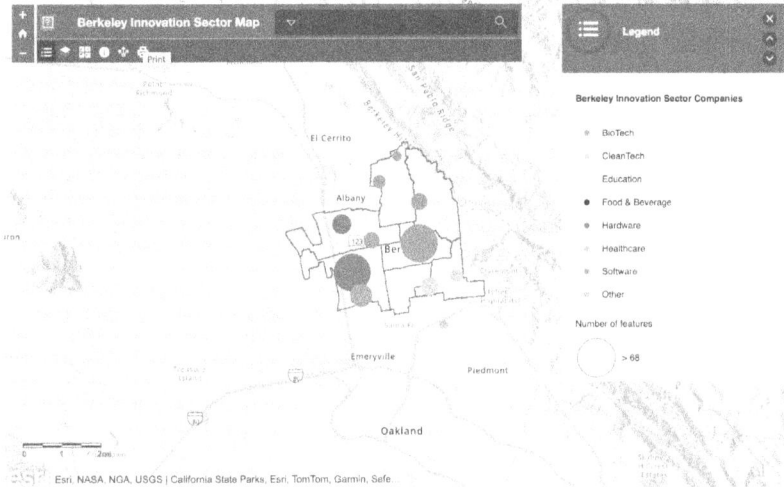

Locations and clusters of innovation companies in the City of Berkeley (SOURCE: BERKELEY STARTUP CLUSTER)

Launched in 2009, the Berkeley Startup Cluster (BSC) collaboration was in many ways an offshoot of the East Bay Green Corridor (EBGC) partnership, which disbanded in 2010. The BSC's goal was to stop Berkeley's "innovation drain," which is a version of the problematic geoeconomic pattern known as brain drain. It's noteworthy that while the EBGC was officialized via a memorandum of understanding between the participating entities, the BSC isn't a legal entity, and its mission isn't officiated by any contractual agreements among its five participating organizations: UC Berkeley, the Lawrence Berkeley National Laboratory, the City of Berkeley, the Berkeley Chamber, and the Downtown Berkeley Association (a property-based business district).

(continued on page 70)

Universities & Cities Drive the Creation of Massive Regional Innovation Ecosystems," December 2016, https://ipira.berkeley.edu/sites/default /files/vortexvswaypointuniversities180823a.pdf.

# Berkeley Lights: Technology Can Take Years to Find a Breakthrough Use

Sometimes the market application for an innovative new technology takes years to identify and even more years to successfully commercialize. That's the moral of the story with a UC Berkeley nanofluidic technology and the startup Berkeley Lights.

Ming C. Wu is a Berkeley professor of electrical engineering and computer science. As of 2024, he was an inventor on thirty-five patents and a serial entrepreneur, having cofounded three companies.[a] In the early 2000s, Wu received US government grants to fund research to "marry nanotechnology with therapeutics" that leveraged his UC lab team's expertise in silicon photonics, optoelectronics, nanophotonics, optical MEMS, and optofluidics. By the mid 2000s that basic research led to

UC Berkeley professor Ming Wu (PHOTO: MARK JOSEPH HANSON)

the development of a nanofluidic technology that uses light to individually control massive amounts of cells.

However, Wu wasn't sure how this innovative optoelectronic cell positioning technology could be applied to real-world problems until a serendipitous lunch meeting years later. Wu had been on the scientific advisory board of the startup FormFactor, which had grown to become the world's leading supplier of advanced wafer probe cards and engineering probe systems. FormFactor went public in 2003, and several years later the company's founder and CEO, Igor Khandros, was on the Berkeley campus taking philosophy classes. During a lunch together at Berkeley's faculty club, Khandros asked Wu about his research. Wu showed his optoelectronic positioning technology. Fortunately, according to Wu, "the technology is very visual. It's recorded. You can see the action on a video clip. So Khandros got enamored with the technology, and figured there had to be some application for it."

Around that time Wu had been talking to several biotech companies to see if they wanted to collaborate on exploring applications of the technology. "The companies were skeptical," Wu said. "They'd ask what the technology was good for.... The companies were thinking in the traditional mode, and asking what biotech steps could the technology replace? But the technology was a whole new approach. So it didn't replace any steps."

Wu and Khandros continued to discuss the optofluidic technology, and in 2011 they launched Berkeley Lights, Inc. (BLI). Khandros was the founding CEO, and Wu took a one-year leave of absence from the university to work full-time at the startup. Wu characterized the EECS department's attitude toward his entrepreneurship adventure as encouraging but hoping that he'd eventually return to his campus faculty position.

BLI launched its operations in a one-story portable building on the western edge of the City of Berkeley along the San Francisco Bay, across from the Golden Gate Bridge. The startup licensed the patent rights from Berkeley and was funded with $4 million from Khandros and his angel investor colleagues.

In search of potential applications, BLI showed a rudimentary demonstration of the optofluidic technology to biotech industry experts, which led to applications in antibody-based drug discovery. By 2013, BLI had a full-scale prototype and in 2016, introduced the first commercial version of a revolutionary platform that enabled functional testing at the single-cell level in a fraction of the time and costs. However, Wu soon learned (what his experienced BLI colleagues had already known) that "it's not easy to disrupt an incumbent technology. The industry's scientists had been using the current technology for decades. They were confident of its efficacy, and anything new needed to be proven against the gold standard. So it took years to measure up to the conventional technology." Eventually BLI's solution was capable of sorting, cloning, culturing, and analyzing antibody secretions of tens of thousands of single cells on a single optofluidic chip, and the platform was on track to be

Instead, these organizations voluntarily collaborate because they realize it's in their mutual best interests to pursue the BSC's goals.

Prior to the town-gown collaborations fostered by the BSC and the EBGC, the relationship between the campus and the City of Berkeley was often adversarial. In fact, the city sued the university in 2005 over the campus's long-range growth plans. At that time the city government also had a reputation of hostility toward corporations, including startup companies. But the EBGC and the BSC mended that ill will, and by the launch of the SkyDeck startup accelerator in 2012, the city-university relationship had become friendly and productive.

used by pharmaceutical companies for antibody discovery, cell line development, and synthetic biology.

In July 2020, during the early peak of the COVID-19 pandemic, BLI went public at a billion-dollar valuation. The company's technology was subsequently used to combat COVID-19, which Wu was especially proud of.[b] After his leave of absence from Berkeley, Wu was a scientific advisor to BLI and remained on its board of directors until the startup's IPO. When Wu returned to Berkeley (heeding the advice from his EECS department colleagues), he subsequently became a Bakar Fellow (profiled in this chapter) based on his research with large-scale silicon photonic switches for data center applications. In 2020, always an entrepreneur, Wu cofounded nEye Systems (with Khandros as an investor and board member) to commercialize that switching technology. ▪

a. In addition to Berkeley Lights, Ming cofounded OMM, Inc. in 1997 to commercialize MEMS optical switches, and nEye Systems, Inc. in 2020 to commercialize silicon photonic MEMS switches.

b. "Researchers Worldwide Are Using Berkeley Lights' Beacon Platform to Combat COVID-19," *PR Newswire,* February 28, 2020, www.prnewswire.com/news-releases/researchers-worldwide-are-using-berkeley-lights-beacon-platform-to-combat-covid-19-301013181.html.

The Berkeley Startup Cluster has a steering committee and a small annual budget funded and managed through the City of Berkeley's Office of Economic Development, which has assumed leadership and coordination responsibilities for the group.[8] The budget mainly supports events, either organized or co-sponsored by the BSC. BSC-organized events include stakeholder feedback forums, themed panel discussions, and an an-

8. As of 2025, Elizabeth Redman Cleveland, the chief strategist for sustainable growth at the City of Berkeley Office of Economic Development, has been leading the BSC since 2018.

nual meeting of BSC advisors who are local startup founders, early-stage investors, commercial real estate developers, and government officials (e.g., the Berkeley mayor) as well as representatives from the five collaborating organizations. The budget also supports the BSC website, communications, and fees to the Berkeley Chamber for serving as the group's fiscal sponsor (and offering it a 501(c)(3) tax status so it can receive philanthropic grants).

**berkeley startup cluster**

The BSC also has provided a channel for local elected officials to garner feedback on City of Berkeley policies and programs that could foster the local innovation ecosystem. The BSC's advocacy has led to many city policy updates, including (1) changing the city's business license policy to exempt startups' philanthropic and government R&D grants (e.g., SBIR and STTR grants) from annual business license taxation; (2) refining the land-use definition of "R&D" to accommodate both office and lab uses; and (3) updating local zoning policy to "Keep Innovation in Berkeley" by simplifying the approval of R&D "use" in the city's commercial corridors.

In 2023 and 2024 the BSC identified approximately four hundred innovation companies (including startups and R&D-intensive established corporations) with addresses in Berkeley. As more startups have located in Berkeley, the BSC's mission matured to "making Berkeley a more vibrant, accessible, and equitable place for startups to launch *and grow.*" In support of those goals, the BSC launched its "Berkeley Ventures, Berkeley Values" initiative, which strives to build a local innovation economy that benefits the whole Berkeley community.

In early 2024 the BSC updated its land use vision and roadmap in recognition that the city's I&E ecosystem (including its variety of office and lab space such as Bakar Labs) was nearing an inflection point. Various R&D-oriented real estate projects were under way that, when viewed holistically and combined with Berkeley's existing innovation assets, could elevate the city's status into a world-class cluster for innovation and startups—distinct from but synergistic with the university's I&E stature.

## First Berkeley Lab-to-Market Course: Cleantech to Market

The Cleantech to Market (C2M) program was conceived in 2008 as an extracurricular pilot project by the technology transfer office at the Lawrence Berkeley National Lab (LBNL) and the Berkeley Energy Resources Collaborative (BERC)—a Berkeley student organization. The idea was to pair multidisciplinary teams of Berkeley students with LBNL scientists who were working on promising clean and green technologies. After the matchmaking, the student teams would research and recommend plans to commercialize those technologies for societal benefit—instead of languishing in labs. Within a year, the C2M pilot program had become so popular with students and scientists, the Energy Institute at Berkeley's Haas School of Business formalized the program as a semester-long course.[9]

In its first year, nearly 120 students applied for C2M's 42 seats. Students were assigned to work on one of ten technologies—half developed at LBNL and the other half developed on the Berkeley campus. Most students were in the business school's MBA program, with a handful coming from Berkeley programs in

---

9. UC Berkeley School of Business professor Catherine Wolfram brought the C2M pilot program into the Energy Institute and hired Beverly Alexander and Cyrus Wadia as the first faculty co-directors.

law, engineering, sciences, and energy and resources. Beverly Alexander, one of the inaugural faculty co-directors of the C2M course, said, "We were very intentional about matching students with technologies. We selected them as if we were creating a company."[10]

During that first C2M class, one example of a technology that a student team worked on was a thin film silicon solar invention (developed by Berkeley researchers Alex Zettl, Marvin Cohen, and Steve Louie). The team developed a fictitious startup company and business model around the technology, which they named Better Silicon. In another example the student team was matched with a communications specification called OpenADR that was developed at LBNL to help buildings save power during peak energy usage times. The team's assignment was to find ways to accelerate the deployment of OpenADR by utilities and their big energy users. The team produced a thirty-five-page report, including a list of the top ten barriers to adoption and suggestions to overcome each barrier. One of the team's recommendations was to launch a third-party nonprofit to focus on outreach.[11] As of 2024, the OpenADR Alliance had over 150 members and more than 200 certified products.

Within a few years of its launch, the Cleantech to Market program had pioneered a new pathway for commercializing the inventions developed at the Lawrence Berkeley National Lab and UC Berkeley. This approach was too time-consuming for many scientists and technology transfer offices to pursue. That led to

10. Julie Chao, "Scientists Benefit as Much as Students from 'Cleantech to Market' Program," Berkeley Lab, May 14, 2010, https://newscenter.lbl .gov/2010/05/14/scientists-benefit-as-much-as-students-from-cleantech-to -market-program/.

11. Chao, "Scientists Benefit as Much as Students from 'Cleantech to Market' Program."

the launch of similar lab-to-market courses (profiled in chapter 4) at the campus that focused on other technology categories. By 2014 the C2M program had become so popular that technology submissions came in from other universities, national labs, and research institutions. "Word had spread," Alexander said. "We hadn't gone outside the Berkeley ecosystem before, but they're coming to us. It has become a nationally competitive process to get technologies into our program."

Also around this time, the C2M program increased the number of projects from the developing world as well as projects from startups. Early on, about 20 percent of the C2M projects had involved startup companies, but by 2014 half of the projects involved startups, and that trend was expected to continue. Alexander characterized C2M as "closer to a startup incubator than a class." She added, "With $CO_2$ levels the highest in human history, the need to develop viable cleantech startups has never been more critical." Brian Steel, a C2M faculty co-director, said, "The program is emblematic of what Berkeley does like no other institution in the world. We have a combination of business and science and engineering expertise here that is second to none."[12]

**C2M** The Strauch Cleantech to Market Program

In 2014 the C2M course culminated with eight teams—made up of thirty-two MBA students and sixteen graduate students from engineering, public policy, chemistry, and other Berkeley schools. The teams presented their results at a symposium that

(continued on page 78)

12. Laura Counts, "Cleantech to Market Expands, Bringing Berkeley Expertise to Other Institutions," *Haas News*, December 16, 2014, https://newsroom .haas.berkeley.edu/cleantech-market-expands-bringing-berkeley-expertise -other-institutions/.

# Zephyrus Biosciences: Leading the Commercializing Process Yourself

As a UC Berkeley bioengineering professor, Amy E. Herr sees creating startups as an essential part of being a scientist in the twenty-first century. "We don't confine ourselves to the lab," she says. "Our goal is to ultimately improve people's lives, so we work to ensure that the technology gets into the hands of the people whose lives we want to improve. Sometimes that means leading the process of commercialization yourself." In 2013 that's what Herr and Kelly Gardner, then a bioengineering PhD student, did when they cofounded Zephyrus Biosciences to commercialize a research tool for single-cell analysis that enables high-resolution biology.

After licensing the intellectual property from Berkeley, in 2014 Zephyrus raised a seed round of $1.5 million from investors that included Mission Bay Capital, then affiliated with QB3. Also in 2014, the startup received $300,000 in grants from the US National Institutes of Health and Berkeley's Bakar Fellows Program (profiled in this chapter). The company launched operations in the QB3 Garage incubator in Berkeley's Stanley Hall.

Zephyrus's first product, called Milo, was a benchtop instrument that allowed researchers to search for specific proteins in about a thousand cells at once. For the first time this enabled the Western Blotting analytic technique to analyze individual cells. The resulting high-throughput and high-selectivity protein fingerprinting gave scientists a way to understand variability within tumors and to deliver new insights into the biology of stem cells, neurology, and human diseases such as cancer.

In 2016, *The Scientist* magazine named Zephyrus's technology a "#1 Innovation." In March of that year the global life sciences company Bio-Techne Corporation acquired Zephyrus. In

UC Berkeley professor Amy Herr (PHOTO BY NOAH BERGER)

response to the acquisition, Gardner said, "We are excited to join Bio-Techne and bring our system into the ProteinSimple family of products. This deal provides an excellent path forward for commercialization of the single cell Western Blot technology. The market reach of Bio-Techne will enable Zephyrus to rapidly reach the broad market of researchers who need to study proteins at the single cell level."[a]

Herr has gone on to serve many I&E leadership and mentorship roles. She was founding director of Berkeley's Bakar BioEnginuity Hub (profiled in chapter 5) and faculty director of Berkeley's Bakar Fellows Program. As of 2025, Herr was vice president of the Chan-Zuckerberg Biohub Network, leading the network's efforts to advance technologies to observe, measure, and analyze human biology in action. ▪

a. "Bio-Techne Corporation Agrees to Acquire Zephyrus Biosciences, Inc.," *PR Newswire*, March 21, 2016, www.prnewswire.com/news-releases/bio-techne -corporation-agrees-to-acquire-zephyrus-biosciences-inc-300238781.html.

attracted some 250 scientists, faculty, alumni, and cleantech business leaders. The winner of the best overall "People's Choice" award was the NearZero Flywheel team, which researched paths to market for a compact, superefficient flywheel battery that can operate in extreme conditions. Other projects included a separator to prevent battery fires in electric vehicles, algorithms to optimize the smart grid, a bioengineered film with energy-generating properties, and ultra-high-efficiency photovoltaics.

By 2018, its tenth year, the C2M program had become a key part of UC Berkeley's I&E ecosystem with a track record of matching more than three hundred researchers and startup founders with Berkeley student teams.[13] And C2M paid off for those cleantech companies (one of which was Mosaic Materials, profiled in chapter 4). Collectively, the C2M startups had raised more than $142 million and employed some three hundred people.[14] An equally important outcome of C2M's experiential learning approach is the students themselves, who graduate savvy about commercializing early-stage technologies. That not only jumpstarts their careers, it also helps propel the larger cleantech mission at Berkeley and beyond.

The C2M program's annual cycle begins in January, when the leadership team winnows down a list of possible startups through meetings with officials from the Department of Energy, the Berkeley-based fellowship program Cyclotron Road (profiled in chapter 4), the Cleantech Open (an accelerator focused on cleantech startups), and the California Energy Commission.

13. By 2018, Beverly Alexander was co-directing C2M with co-director Brian Steel and C2M faculty member Bill Shelander, a trio affectionately known as "B3" for their first names. Alexander retired from C2M in 2020.

14. Kim Girard, "Cleantech to Market Celebrates Ten Years," *Haas News*, November 29, 2018, https://newsroom.haas.berkeley.edu/cleantech-to-market-program-celebrates-10-successful-years-at-haas/.

Beverly Alexander and Brian Steel celebrate the 10th year of the C2M program
(PHOTO: JIM BLOCK)

Steel said, "It really helps to have knowledgeable partners who refer pre-vetted technologies." Student teams are chosen in April and May, and projects kick off in August, culminating with presentations at a year-end symposium and reports that assess the technologies and recommend paths to market.

As of 2025, more than five hundred graduate students have completed the C2M fifteen-week course. C2M has become a marquis program that has forged alliances with California state agencies, such as the California Energy Commission, and US federal agencies including the Department of Energy, as well as many top universities and startup incubators. Reflecting on the C2M trajectory, Alexander said, "We've gone from a local pilot to a national pipeline. And our alumni are among the 'who's who' of the cleantech industry."

## First Berkeley Startup Accelerator: SkyDeck

Around 2011 the novel concept that a nonprofit university—especially a *public*, nonprofit university—should establish a startup accelerator to help for-profit companies launch and grow was controversial and even ludicrous to some in the university community. A university program that supports startups (1) wasn't obviously consistent with the university's research and education mission, (2) could lead to university financial conflicts of interests, (3) could enable the use of a university's resources for personal private gain, and (4) might even risk disqualifying a university's nonprofit tax status.

Following the 2008 recession, 2011 was another year of budget austerity for UC Berkeley. Existing campus programs faced additional budget cuts. Consequently, when Mike Alvarez Cohen conceived of converting the downtown Berkeley lab that Intel was shutting down into a startup accelerator, he assumed that proposing the campus to fund it would be rejected for financial and policy reasons. Accordingly, Cohen's original $150,000 operating plan for the SkyDeck accelerator was based on (1) sponsorship funds from startup service providers (such as venture capital funds and law firms), (2) fully furnished office equipment donated and left behind by Intel, (3) below-market compensation for the accelerator's management (with the potential for income from stock equity in startups participating in the accelerator program), and (4) discounted lease rates from the building's ownership, which had ties to Berkeley.[15] The operating plan only sought minor temporary launch funds from Berkeley's EECS de-

15. David Teece was a major shareholder of the company that owned the building at 2150 Shattuck Avenue, and he was also a professor in UC Berkeley's Haas School of Business and on the board of the school's Institute for Business Innovation.

partment or College of Engineering of about $1,000 per month for the first year.[16]

Despite those low expectations, the proposal for a startup accelerator in the city's tallest building on the entire 10,000-square-foot penthouse floor with 360-degree views, including of the Golden Gate Bridge, San Francisco, and the Berkeley campus—and only a block from the campus—resonated with the EECS department chair and the College of Engineering's dean and associate dean.[17] As a result, SkyDeck's operating plan was changed to become a campus-wide collaboration led by Berkeley's College of Engineering, School of Business, and vice chancellor for research's office. Correspondingly, the budget was changed based on the College of Engineering and School of Business each contributing $150,000 and the vice chancellor for research's office contributing $125,000.

Still, the university's involvement in a startup accelerator encountered resistance until two realizations gained momentum: (1) an accelerator would further the university's mission of education by providing exceptional experiential learning opportunities for Berkeley students and recent graduates to develop entrepreneurship skills—regardless of whether their startups succeeded or failed; and (2) an accelerator could advance the

*(continued on page 83)*

16. Mike Alvarez Cohen, who worked in UC Berkeley's Office of Technology Licensing and was a cofounder of the Berkeley Startup Cluster, conceived the SkyDeck accelerator and authored its proposal and operating plan.

17. The EECS department chair was David Culler. The College of Engineering dean was Shankar Sastry, the associate dean was Tsu-Jae King Liu (who subsequently became the college's dean), the School of Business dean was Rich Lyons (who subsequently became Berkeley's first chief innovation & entrepreneurship officer and in 2024, Berkeley's twelfth chancellor).

# Amplifying Access to STEM and Entrepreneurship Pathways: Cal NERDS

During Dr. Andrew Ekelem's sophomore year at UC Berkeley, he suffered a snowboarding accident that changed his life. But with the help of the university's Cal NERDS program and faculty mentors, Ekelem embraced his entrepreneurial spirit, switched his major to bioengineering, and focused his purpose on rehabilitation and using his engineering talents to help others.

Established in 2005, Cal NERDS has a variety of STEM programs, a STEM student center, and a comprehensive online STEM resource hub (star.berkeley.edu). Cal NERDS's support for Ekelem through the UC LEADS pre-PhD program enabled him to conduct research at UC Irvine—closer to his hometown—while he underwent medical treatment for his injury. After intensive physical therapy, Ekelem returned to Berkeley and participated in a Cal NERDS–funded internship in the exoskeleton lab of Berkeley professor Homayoon Kazerooni (profiled in chapter 2). During that time Ekelem prototyped a new wheelchair, using a novel mechanism for levered propulsion. He went on to earn a PhD in mechanical engineering.

Fast forward to 2024, Ekelem is chief product officer of Evolution Devices, founded in 2017 by Pierluigi Mantovani and Juan M. Rodriguez, both

Andrew Ekelem with EvoWalk device

Berkeley alumni. The company's first product is an FDA-approved device called EvoWalk, a wearable medical device that detects the phase of walking of the wearer in order to send the appropriate electrostimulation. The device helps people with neurological injuries improve their mobility by strengthening their movements.

As of 2025, Ekelem continues to stay connected to Cal NERDS by giving keynote talks and interacting with undergraduates. His entrepreneurial energy is a natural part of Berkeley, which aligns with Cal NERDS's emphasis on exposure, participation, and transformation. Ekelem's innovative problem-solving, resilience, and dedication to improving the human condition, especially for people with disabilities, is a prime example of how Cal NERDS and others contribute to Berkeley's I&E excellence. ▪

university's mission of societal impact by helping university startups commercialize the innovations from Berkeley research.

In mid-2011 the two deans and the vice chancellor for research established a memorandum of understanding and approved the SkyDeck plan. Soon after, the Berkeley Chancellor's Community Fund awarded SkyDeck a $50,000 grant (divided into $25,000 over two years), the Lawrence Berkeley National Lab provided a $25,000 grant, and the City of Berkeley's Office of Economic Developed also provided a $25,000 grant.[18] In the spring of 2012, SkyDeck welcomed its first cohort of Berkeley startup teams, and within three years, SkyDeck became a flagship program in Berkeley's I&E ecosystem.

18. The LBNL grant was approved by Paul Alivisatos, who was the LBNL executive director and subsequently UC Berkeley's vice chancellor for research and then executive vice chancellor and provost.

## Funding Translational Research and Entrepreneurship: Bakar Fellows Program

Advancing basic research with promising potential for societal impact can be impeded by a lack of funding for translational research, proof-of-concept R&D, and entrepreneurship support. To address that impediment, the Bakar Fellows Program was launched in 2012 to accelerate important research discoveries out of UC Berkeley labs for the benefit of society.[19] For Berkeley faculty with promising projects that are more advanced than basic research, but not quite to the point of commercialization, the Bakar program awards funding and entrepreneurship support to mature and commercialize their ground-breaking innovations.

Bakar provides support via the Bakar Award and the Bakar Prize. Through a competitive application process, winning faculty members are designated as Bakar Faculty Fellows and provided with Bakar Award funding to achieve established milestones and advance their research concepts toward commercialization. As they near successful completion of a Bakar Award project, Faculty Fellows whose technologies continue to show promise are invited to apply for a Bakar Prize. The prize funding can be used over several years to bridge from proof-of-concept work to startup commercialization.

In 2017 the Bakar Fellows Program launched its Innovation Fellows Capitalize Program in recognition that bringing research to market is a team effort. Innovation Fellows are entrepreneurially inclined graduate students or postdocs working with a Bakar Faculty Fellow. Many Innovation Fellows are ex-

19. The Bakar Fellows Program was made possible by philanthropic funding from the Bakar Foundation.

ploring entrepreneurship for the first time and, accordingly, enrichment activities and events are a core component of this program. In 2023 the Bakar Fellows Program introduced its Ignite Scholars Program, which provides undergraduate students with a stipend to work with Bakar Fellows in their labs. New cohorts of exceptional undergraduates are chosen every semester.

Academic Innovation Catalyst (AIC) teamed up with the Bakar Fellows Program in 2024 to offer the AIC-Bakar Award. For Berkeley faculty developing technology to solve climate-related issues, the award provides up to $300,000 over three years to further develop the technology and explore its commercial potential. As of 2025, the Bakar Fellows Program

B Bakar Fellows Program

supported eighty-four Faculty Fellows (from sixteen academic departments), ninety Innovation Fellows (graduate students, postdocs, and project scientists), and twenty-four Ignite Scholars (undergraduates). The program has catalyzed more than twenty startups.

## Leveraging Postdoctoral Talent: Berkeley Postdocs Entrepreneurship Program

In 2024, UC Berkeley had more than thirteen hundred postdoctoral researchers on campus, pursuing the next step in their career trajectories, after having completed their PhD programs. The conventional path for most postdocs is to go on to university faculty or industry positions. However, an increasing number of those accomplished scholars are curious about or drawn to entrepreneurship and startup opportunities. To address this talent pool's entrepreneurship potential, in 2011 the Berkeley Postdoc Entrepreneurship Program (BPEP) was launched to foster en-

trepreneurship among Berkeley's postdocs, graduate students, and visiting scholars, through awareness of the career path, educational workshops, and hands-on advisory opportunities with Berkeley startups.

At the outset the amount of campus community interest in BPEP was uncertain. So it took persistence from the program's founder, Naresh Sunkara (who was a Berkeley postdoc at the time of the program's inception), to convince Berkeley's vice chancellor for research office and Berkeley's Visiting Scholar and Postdoc Affairs (VSPA) office to support BPEP. Most BPEP events are held around dinnertime, when grad students and postdocs typically end their workday. Initially the VSPA office provided some funding for food and beverages, but BPEP's meal expenses have been funded mostly by sponsorships from law firms and venture capital funds.

Under Sunkara's leadership, BPEP has supported the launch of numerous successful startups. The program's workshops were the first step before launching startups for many Berkeley founders at such companies as Catena Biosciences, Kapacity, Bacchus Therapeutics, X-Therma, and Nelumbos. Those stories exemplify BPEP's effectiveness in driving Berkeley's I&E excellence by empowering postdocs and graduate students to pursue entrepreneurship career paths and translate their research into products with societal impact. In 2020 BPEP was augmented with the PostX program, a set of I&E resources for postdocs.

# FOUR

# Fostering an Ecosystem Boom

You can't use up creativity.
The more you use, the more you have.

—■ MAYA ANGELOU

## Berkeley I&E, 2013–2018

Galvanized by UC Berkeley's leaders championing entrepreneur-ship and startups, around 2013 a culture that valued the passion of entrepreneurs and the excitement of startups spread across Berkeley's STEM community. That spurred a surge in new I&E programs on and near the campus. Berkeley's I&E ecosystem became exuberant.

As with many top US research universities, management on the Berkeley campus is relatively distributed across its commit-tees, colleges, schools, departments, and faculty labs. Berkeley has a tradition of shared governance by which faculty share responsibility for the campus's management (while preserving the authority of the university's governing board, the Regents, to set policy).[1] Accordingly, Berkeley's central administrative

---

1. "Shared Governance at the University of California: An Historical Re-view," Berkeley Public Policy The Goldman School, publications, https://gspp.berkeley.edu/research-and-impact/publications/shared-governance-at-the-university-of-california-an-historical-review.

leadership doesn't aim to control most departmental decisions. So, not surprisingly, Berkeley's boom in I&E activity was also not centrally coordinated. Instead, the ecosystem blossomed organically.[2] The uncoordinated surge was also fueled by Berkeley's culture of giving faculty, students, and staff the agency to independently establish extracurricular programs that address campus opportunities and solve campus problems—for example, insufficient support for the burgeoning student interests in entrepreneurship. Moreover, Berkeley's I&E surge was itself entrepreneurial, with many programs thriving, others pivoting to gain traction, and some eventually shutting down.

By the end of 2018 there was at least one (and often more than one) Berkeley program for practically every phase of a startup journey, including ideation, formation, incubation, acceleration, and scaling. The range of programs not only spanned the startup journey but also market sectors such as information technology, biotechnology, health tech, cleantech, fintech (e.g., blockchain), social (nonprofit) ventures, and more. By some definitions, Berkeley had nearly a hundred I&E-related programs. That led to a large increase in I&E capacity and an increase in ecosystem complexity and redundancy. This was evident with the launch of several startup accelerator programs, lab-to-market courses, and Berkeley-centric venture capital funds. Most of those initia-

2. Interestingly, a similar uncoordinated I&E surge occurred at MIT in the 2010s as documented in Jean-Jacques Degroof, *From the Basement to the Dome: How MITs Unique Culture Created a Thriving Entrepreneurial Community* (Cambridge, MA: MIT Press, 2021). For more information on these university I&E patterns, see Mike Cohen, "Strategies for Developing University Innovation Ecosystems: An Analysis, Segmentation, and Strategic Framework Based on Somewhat Non-Intuitive and Slightly Controversial Findings," Office of Intellectual Property & Industry Research Alliances (IPIRA), UC Berkeley, https://ipira.berkeley.edu/sites/default/files/strategies_for_developing_university_innovation_ecosystems_2016_sept_les_nouvelles.pdf.

tives had a distinct focus and approach, but there was overlap, competition, and confusion.

Not surprisingly, this period of exuberance raised the question, Can too much unaligned campus activity cause counterproductive or suboptimal outcomes? Berkeley's response to that question was key to its continued I&E momentum. By 2014 a perception was growing among several Berkeley administrative leaders, entrepreneurial faculty, and influential alumni that while Berkeley was spinning out many successful startups and establishing many beneficial I&E programs, the campus was still not doing enough to coordinate the entrepreneurship programs or foster the success of its startups (especially compared to some peer universities).[3]

In 2015 that spreading consensus inspired the vice chancellor for research to convene a group of Berkeley faculty, students, staff, and alumni to meet biweekly to discuss the activities of the dynamic ecosystem.[4] A year later, that group was formalized as the campus's I&E Council (profiled in this chapter).

Also in 2015, the consensus concerning the complexity of the campus's I&E ecosystem led Berkeley's intellectual property management and licensing office to expand its website with content to help people navigate the vast I&E resources. Two years later, that content was redeveloped and relaunched as BEGIN (Berkeley Gateway to Innovation, begin.berkeley.edu, profiled in this chapter)—the campus's first official online portal for its I&E ecosystem.

Berkeley executive leadership's advocacy for entrepreneurship gained momentum in March 2016, with the appointment

3. See the faculty-led report "Entrepreneurship at UC Berkeley," published in 2018.

4. Graham Flemming was the vice chancellor for research from 2009 to 2015.

of Professor Paul Alivisatos as the vice chancellor for research and several months later as the executive vice chancellor and provost (EVCP)—Berkeley's second highest leadership position. In addition to being an award-winning scientist, Alivisatos was a serial entrepreneur, having been involved with creating three companies.[5] Alivisatos's enthusiasm for startups was based on his experience that "his engagement with the world of entrepreneurship did not just follow research in his lab. In fact, it greatly enriched his academic work."[6] Following Alivisatos's promotion to EVCP, the campus's next two vice chancellors of research, Randy Katz (2017–21) and Kathy Yelick (starting in 2021), were both EECS faculty—Berkeley's most entrepreneurship-oriented department.[7]

In the last quarter of 2016 the EVCP convened a series of dinner meetings (profiled later in this chapter) attended by about a dozen faculty and staff who were Berkeley I&E leaders. The EVCP described the meetings as the first in a "process which is very important to the future of the campus—refining our strategy with respect to the campus involvement in, and support of, faculty and student engagement with entrepreneurship initiatives."

To help frame and stir the discussion in the dinner series, one of the participants, David Teece, authored a paper in which

5. In addition to his research excellence and serial entrepreneurship, Paul Alivisatos had been the head of the Lawrence Berkeley National Lab from 2009 to 2016. During that time he had a leadership role with the East Bay Green Corridor and approved LBNL's $25,000 grant to support the launch of the SkyDeck startup accelerator.

6. "Bear Perspective: A Scholar's Journey into Entrepreneurship," *UC Berkeley Inspire,* https://inspire.berkeley.edu/p/promise-winter-2017/bear -perspective-scholars-journey-entrepreneurship/.

7. Randy Katz was a contributor to the UC Berkeley EECS department's RAID and Ingres project, which led to the founding of several companies, including Relational, Informix, and Sybase.

he observed that "parts of the campus have been lukewarm (some might say even hostile) to commercialization of faculty research."[8] He also noted that "despite encouragement at the Office of the President and at the chancellor level, the historical record indicates that UCB faculty (with the important exceptions of electrical engineering, computer sciences, and recently biological sciences) have been only somewhat entrepreneurial. Except in isolated pockets, the campus culture remains ambivalent."

Those dinner discussions motivated the EVCP to commission a faculty-led research report titled "Entrepreneurship at UC Berkeley." That report was published in 2018, and among its findings, the report recommended a new administrative position called the chief innovation and entrepreneurship officer to help Berkeley's I&E ecosystem achieve its full potential. The staffing of that new position in July 2019 marked the start of the next phase in Berkeley's I&E trajectory.

▪ ▪ ▪ ▪ ▪

## More Entrepreneurship Curricula

### Lab-to-Market Courses

A university can be an ideal ecosystem for teaching entrepreneurship skills via hands-on, real-world learning by enabling students to explore business strategies for a university's scientific discoveries and technological innovations. This ideal ecosystem is based on a university's ample supply of two resources:

(continued on page 94)

8.  David Teece was a professor in UC Berkeley's School of Business and on the board of the school's Institute for Business Innovation. David J. Teece, "Managing UC Berkeley in the 21st Century: Campus Research, (Social) Innovation, and Entrepreneurship," Hass School of Business, UC Berkeley, October 25, 2016, https://haas.berkeley.edu/wp-content/uploads/RebuildingBerkeleyfor21stCentury.pdf.

# 4D Molecular Therapeutics: Delivering Gene Therapy Cures

David Schaffer is a UC Berkeley professor of chemical and biomolecular engineering, bioengineering, and molecular and cell biology. He is an inventor on more than fifty patents and a serial entrepreneur, having cofounded eight companies as of 2024.[a]

According to Schaffer, the old joke in the field of gene therapy is that there are only three problems with gene therapy: delivery, delivery, delivery. That inspired him and cofounder David Kirn to spin out 4D Molecular Therapeutics (4DMT) in 2013, based on directed evolution technology used in Schaffer's lab to solve the problem of gene therapy delivery. 4DMT licensed the patent rights from Berkeley and built a proprietary Therapeutic Vector Evolution platform to develop adeno-associated viruses (AAV) vectors and related gene therapies. The startup initially targeted cures for blinding diseases ranging from inherited defects like retinitis pigmentosa to degenerative illnesses of old age, such as macular degeneration.

Schaffer met Kirn during an event at QB3 (profiled in chapter 2), a University of California hub for innovation and entre-

UC Berkeley professor David Schaffer

preneurship in the life sciences. Getting to know each other, they determined they had a lot in common. Kirn, a biotechnology entrepreneur and physician-scientist, had already co-founded a number of startups as well as consulted on clinical development programs. "Working with David has been fruitful," Schaffer said. "I've been able to come up-to-speed on the business side of developing startups along with working with him on clinical trials."[b]

4DMT began operating in the QB3 Garage incubator. The company's first hire was Melissa Kotterman, who had prior experience with Schaffer as a graduate student in his lab where she worked on the gene therapy technology that the university licensed to 4DMT.[c] In 2019, Kotterman said, "I think it is very rare for a graduate student to have a direct opportunity, so quickly out of graduate school, to see their research really be translated, able to help patients in a really, really, rapid way."[h] Now a serial entrepreneur and investor, Kotterman advises new founders in the QB3 mentoring program.

In a 2019 interview Schaffer discussed how he manages both his lab and multiple startups: "My lab is always going to be my priority, but that said, being able to work with companies has really benefited the lab in a couple of ways. It has taught me about the next steps of drug development, and that has helped the way that I shape the research in our lab. And it has also really motivated the people in the lab—I can say that something a graduate student created a few years ago is in a human clinical trial."[b] In December 2020, 4DMT raised $193 million in its initial public offering that valued the company at about $500 million. As of 2025, 4DMT has grown into a clinical-stage biopharma company developing therapies that unlock the full potential of genetic therapy to treat a range of diseases.

When asked what advice he has for up-and-coming young entrepreneurial scientists, Schaffer said: "It's important to learn across fields. You need to figure out how to 'speak' both science and business. You can consider a multi-disciplinary approach, which could mean taking classes outside your major or doing research across fields. UC Berkeley recognizes the need for such training and now offers simultaneous degree programs that allow students to study both science and business, but nothing can replace the hands-on experience of starting a new company."[b] ∎

a. In addition to 4D Molecular Therapeutics, other companies that Schaffer cofounded include Axent Biosciences, Ignite Immunotherapy (acquired by Pfizer), Rewrite Therapeutics (acquired by Intellia), and Valitor.

b. Marge D'Wylde, "The College of Chemistry and the Startup Culture," *Catalyst Magazine* (Spring/Summer 2019), 15, https://escholarship.org/uc/item/6t84c4sd.

c. In 2024, Melissa Kotterman joined David Schaffer's most recent startup as the company's CEO.

(1) an annual cycle of new students who are eager to learn entrepreneurship skills, and (2) an ongoing stream of discoveries and innovations that have the potential for commercial success and societal benefit. When those two resources are coupled with faculty who provide engaging curriculum, dynamic class environments, and experienced entrepreneurship coaching, then a university has all the required assets to offer popular lab-to-market (L2M) courses.

With an abundance of those assets at UC Berkeley, it's not surprising that over the decade following the 2008 launch of the Cleantech to Market lab-to-market course (profiled in chapter 3), several other L2M courses have sprung up in various campus departments. Each L2M course has differentiated itself by either its teaching method, technology

C2M — The Strauch Cleantech to Market Program

sector focus, source of technologies, or student acceptance requirements. As of 2024, Berkeley's variety of L2M courses include the following (listed in order of launch):

- **IP to Market in the College of Engineering.** This course focuses on university patents with commercial potential but an unclear commercialization strategy. For example, whether the optimal plan is to license the intellectual property to an established corporation or spin out a startup. The course was launched in 2011 by Berkeley IEOR professor Lee Flemming along with Matthew Rappaport and Bowman Heide.

- **New Product Development in the College of Chemistry.** This course focuses on new product development and commercialization, including within established corporations or by startups launching their initial product. The course (under the Berkeley College of Chemistry's Professional Masters Degree in Product Development) was launched in 2013 and taught by Dr. Keith Alexander.

- **Lean Transfer in the School of Business.** This course targets many students who want to learn startup entrepreneurship skills via a hands-on course but don't have their own business idea or technology to work on. So the course couples those students with university researchers working on technologies that need commercialization assessments. The course was launched in 2017 by Rhonda Shrader, the executive director of the entrepreneurship programs in Berkeley's School of Business, and Errol Arkilic (who was previously the founder and lead program director for the NSF I-Corps program). As of 2024, students were typically a mix of MBA students as well as masters and PhD students in the STEM fields. Inventors explain their technologies to the students. If a technology is selected, the inventor serves as a mentor to the team, but the students do all the work of talking to potential customers, partners, and competitors as they search for product-market fit. No business experience is needed. Teams are just required to "get out of the classroom" and conduct at least eighty customer interviews during the semester.

▪ **NSF I-Corps Northern California Hub.** In 2011 the US National Science Foundation (NSF) launched the Innovation Corps (I-Corps) to augment NSF's mission by using a customer discovery process that enables research teams to quickly assess their technology's market potential. I-Corps prepares scientists and engineers to extend their focus beyond the lab to increase the economic and societal impact of NSF-funded basic research projects.

In 2017 the NSF expanded and reorganized its I-Corps program to include a new regional structure called I-Corps Hubs. UC Berkeley was selected as the host campus for the San Francisco Bay Area I-Corps Hub (which encompasses UC San Francisco and Stanford).

As of 2024, Berkeley's I-Corps Hub trains early-stage teams with a fundamental technology or engineering innovation to find a scalable business model through the customer discovery process. During the free one-week immersive course with three remote evening sessions, teams learn from proven entrepreneurs how to conduct fifteen customer feedback interviews, identify top customer segments and value propositions, and find product-market fit. Teams that complete the Berkeley regional I-Corps program may be eligible to continue to the seven-week national NSF I-Corps program, which includes a nondilutive $50,000 NSF grant.

In 2024, NSF chose UC Berkeley's I-Corps program as the lead for the new United States Northwest regional I-Corps Hub (which also includes Oregon State University, University of Alaska–Fairbanks, UC Davis, UC Irvine, UC San Francisco, UC Santa Cruz, and University of Washington).

### Entrepreneurship Dual Degree Programs

In addition to the various lab-to-market courses, UC Berkeley established two dual degree programs that emphasize entrepreneurship.

In 2017, Berkeley's School of Business and College of Engineering launched the Management, Entrepreneurship & Technology (MET) program.[9] This joint bachelor of science degree program integrates engineering and business curricula with the mindset of entrepreneurship. MET provides students with professional development, internship opportunities, and company excursions. In tandem, students receive the same high-caliber Berkeley courses as students pursuing degrees in aerospace engineering, bioengineering, civil and environmental engineering, electrical engineering computer sciences, industrial engineering operations research, materials science engineering, mechanical engineering, and business administration.

In 2020 the Haas School of Business and the College of Let-

---

9. The Berkeley MET program was made possible by philanthropic funding from UC Berkeley alumni Janelle Grimes and Michael Grimes.

ters and Science launched the Robinson Life Science, Business, and Entrepreneurship (LSBE) Program.[10] This dual degree program enables students to earn a bachelor of science in business administration and a bachelor of arts in molecular and cell biology, integrative biology, or neuroscience. LSBE offers specialized coursework taught by expert faculty, networking opportunities, personalized career coaching, and mentoring opportunities within a small peer-to-peer cohort of students who aspire to become future leaders and innovators in the life sciences.

## More Incubators and Accelerators

Startup accelerators (for brevity, in this section the phrase "startup accelerators" also includes startup incubator programs) are key to the success of many founding teams. And there's no better entity for a startup accelerator to affiliate and colocate with than a university that has a vibrant entrepreneurship culture. The affiliation and colocation are a win-win boost to the accelerator and university communities.

For a university, an accelerator program provides entrepreneurship-oriented students with exciting experiential learning opportunities—regardless of whether a startup succeeds or fails. And for the majority of university spinouts that don't immediately have venture capital funding, experienced management, and private R&D space, an accelerator program offers the founders guidance from advisors, access to investors, and office space. Plus, co-incubating with other founders provides camaraderie and the opportunity to learn from others' entrepreneurial experiences. Additionally, the accelerator can leverage

10. The Berkeley LSBE program was made possible by philanthropic funding from UC Berkeley alumni Mark and Stephanie Robinson.

the university's (1) deal flow of spinouts, (2) entrepreneurship courses and events, (3) faculty interested in consulting, (4) students looking for internships, (5) recent graduates searching for startup ideas and cofounders, (6) R&D facilities that companies can share, and (7) successful alumni with a pay-it-back mindset.

In the years following the 2012 launch of the SkyDeck startup accelerator (profiled in this chapter as well as chapter 3), the decentralized exuberance of Berkeley's I&E ecosystem led to several other startup accelerators on and near the campus. As of 2024, Berkeley's startup accelerators included SkyDeck, the CITRIS Foundry, UC Launch, StEP, Free Ventures, Entrepreneurs at Berkeley (E@B), Xcelerator, and Cyclotron Road.

### CITRIS Foundry

Following the success of the QB3 startup accelerator and incubator program at UC San Francisco, the CITRIS organization at UC Berkeley launched the Foundry startup accelerator in 2013. The CITRIS Foundry's inaugural program recruited and nurtured deep tech startups (defined as those that require a great deal of R&D development time and capital-intensive R&D resources to commercialize their products) across a wide range of information technology–related areas. Teams received weekly coaching and connections to startup resources such as legal, banking, and funding services.

Notably, the Foundry pioneered the university's approach of an accelerator obtaining stock equity (2 percent) in its startups as fair market compensation to the university in return for the startups' use of university resources for private benefit. Future income from the startup equity was also intended to eventually fund the

*(continued on page 102)*

## Mosaic Materials:
## Novel Materials for Carbon Capture

While completing his PhD at UC Berkeley's College of Chemistry, Tom McDonald had planned to become a professor.[a] He even had a postdoc position lined up at Imperial College London and had told his landlord that he was moving to the UK. But then, McDonald's PhD advisor, Professor Jeffrey Long, and another student in Long's lab, Steven Kaye, convinced McDonald to join them as the cofounding CEO in a startup to commercialize the technology that they had been developing. That's how the Berkeley spinout Mosaic Materials was born in 2015. In a 2022 interview with the research fellowship program Activate, McDonald stated, "I considered it long and hard—it was a really close decision between Mosaic and academia. I ended up saying, 'Well if I don't do this, the technology is gonna die. So yes, I'll do it."

When he started his graduate work at Berkeley, McDonald joined a research group that was part of the Center for Gas Separations—one of the US Department of Energy's Frontier Research Centers. The research group was exploring how metal-organic frameworks (MOFs) could be used to make gas separations more energy efficient and affordable. "I had wanted to work on climate technology ever since reading Al Gore's book when I was in eighth grade," McDonald said. "So I said 'sign me up.' It was only my third day at Berkeley and I already knew I'd be working on carbon capture using MOFs and I basically did that for the next thirteen years."

While experimenting with unusual and controversial approaches to functionalizing MOFs, the Berkeley researchers invented an MOF material that exhibited exceptional carbon dioxide absorption properties, including the ability to pull carbon directly out of the air. That technology was licensed by Mosaic

Mosaic Materials cofounder and CEO Tom McDonald (left) and UC Berkeley professor Jeff Long (right) (CREDIT: MOSAIC MATERIALS)

and became the startup's core focus. One of Mosaic's first wins was when McDonald and Kaye were accepted into the Activate program (then called Cyclotron Road, as profiled in chapter 4) at the Lawrence Berkeley National Lab. The paid two-year fellowship enabled McDonald and Kaye to focus full-time on R&D and building the company.

Mosaic's carbon capture material was promising, but back around 2015 few investors were interested in funding the startup. So initially the cofounders looked to government grants for funding to derisk the technology and lower its costs. "So much of the story of Mosaic has been about help along the way by a lot of amazing government sponsors," McDonald said. The first of those sponsors was the California Energy Commission, which funded Mosaic to investigate using its MOFs to drive down the cost of biogas production. "That funding was a critical lifeline—along with the Activate fellowship," McDonald recalled.

The US Navy and NASA were other important government sponsors. Each took an interest in how Mosaic's technology could improve carbon dioxide removal for life support within submarines and spacecraft, respectively. The Department of Energy (DOE) had also been a key supporter, going back to the early research at Berkeley and then through grants that Mosaic was awarded through the DOE's Small Business Innovation Research (SBIR) program, ARPA-E, and Advanced Manufacturing Office (which also funds Activate fellowships).

At that time, Mosaic connected with the energy technology corporation Baker Hughes. That interaction culminated in 2022 with Baker Hughes's acquisition of Mosaic to advance next-generation carbon dioxide capture technology to overcome climate change. Baker Hughes was drawn to Mosaic because the Berkeley spinout's technology requires less energy to operate, provides a low total cost of ownership, and it can be used across energy and industrial sectors, including refining, aviation, shipping, municipalities, steel, and cement manufacturing.

Foundry's operations. Three years later, in 2016, the university officially established a policy to accept stock equity in return for use of the university's incubator and accelerator programs.[11]

11. The Foundry's stock equity agreement with startups was developed in 2013 by Mike Alvarez Cohen in UC Berkeley's Office of Intellectual Property and Industry Research Alliances. Three years later, in 2016, the University of California established a policy for accepting stock in return for incubator and accelerator resources. See "Guidelines on Accepting and Managing Equity in Return for Access to University Facilities and/or Services," July 1, 2016, ucop.edu/innovation-transfer-operations/_files/Accepting%20Equity/UC%20Accepting%20Equity%20guidelines.pdf.

In 2022, Activate's CEO Ilan Gur stated: "It's been such a pleasure and an honor to support Mosaic over the past six years. The team's personal focus on driving climate impact is inspiring. The cofounders were intent on proving that MOFs were more than fanciful academic chemistry but could be powerful tools for carbon capture. The Baker Hughes acquisition is a great step forward for the company and for meeting the urgent need for effective carbon removal technology."

In 2024, Baker Hughes launched a collaborative research initiative with Berkeley to further develop carbon capture technologies.[b] This exemplifies the virtuous cycle of how Berkeley's I&E ecosystem and government-sponsored research lead to innovative technologies, startup companies, and solutions to societal problems such as climate change. •

a. The source for much of this content is from "Startup to Sale: How Cohort 2015 Fellow Tom McDonald Built and Sustained Mosaic Materials," *Activate*, May 10, 2022, www.activate.org/news/mosaic-materials-sold-baker-hughes -tom-mcdonald.

b. "Baker Hughes and the University of California, Berkeley, Establish Global Decarbonization Research Institute," press release, December 12, 2024, www .bakerhughes.com/company/news/baker-hughes-and-university-california -berkeley-establish-global-decarbonization.

In 2019 the Foundry pivoted its program to focus on student founders instead of startup companies. That change enabled the program to serve a larger student population. In 2024 that approach was expanded to include faculty researching readily commercializable technologies aligned with CITRIS's research initiatives primarily in AI, information technology, aerospace, climate, and health. As of 2025, the Foundry has supported over 400 students, working on more than 135 ventures that have raised over $220 million in funding.

## UC LAUNCH

Built on the popularity of the former Berkeley Business Plan Competition, but rejecting the "beauty contest" aspect of a pure pitch competition, UC LAUNCH accepted its first cohort in 2015. The program was founded by Andre Marquis, a former executive director of Berkeley's Lester Center for Entrepreneurship (profiled in chapter 1), and subsequently led by Rhonda Shrader, who followed Marquis as the executive director of the entrepreneurship programs in Berkeley's School of Business.

While based on the Berkeley campus, the program accepts students, faculty, and alumni startups from all ten campuses of the University of California. LAUNCH uses a rigorous three-month curriculum that goes beyond the traditional lean startup methodology by focusing on metrics and the skills a startup needs to scale everything from operations to sales.

## StEP

The startup incubator Student Entrepreneurship Program (StEP) was launched in 2018 as part of a reboot of the student organization Berkeley Entrepreneurs Association (BEA). BEA members run StEP in coordination with the School of Business's entrepreneurship program. The ten-week program of weekly two-hour sessions culminates in a showcase event to an audience that includes a panel of investors. The program is available to Berkeley students in all degree programs and permanent faculty, but it's targeted at early-stage startup

founders. Accordingly, many StEP teams go on to participate in later-stage programs such as LAUNCH and SkyDeck. As of 2025, StEP has helped some 300 student founders working on more than 100 early-stage startups raise over $16 million in funding.

### Free Ventures

Launched in 2013, Free Ventures is a pre-seed accelerator that elevates early-stage student startups to the next level by combining the power of its mentor network, sponsor-led curriculum, and personalized structure. The semester-long accelerator program operates a cohort of four to five startups

in spring and fall. As of 2025, Free Ventures has helped hundreds of teams raise more than $200 million in venture capital. Many of its startup teams have gone on to accelerator programs such as SkyDeck and Y Combinator.

### Entrepreneurs at Berkeley

The student organization Entrepreneurs at Berkeley (E@B) provides various services, including a ten-week startup incubator program. The program teaches first-time founders the foundational principles of entrepreneurship and guides innovators from the initial concept to pitching to top-tier VCs and accelerators. The cur-

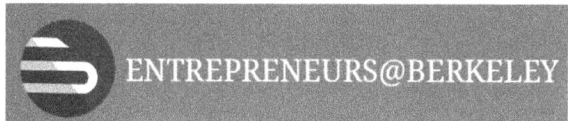

riculum, resources, and workshops equip founders with the tools and exposure necessary to gain traction and grow further. Leveraging its partnerships with venture capital firms and accelerator programs, E@B's incubator program hosts speaker panels, pitching sessions, and networking events to gain exposure to professional connections, feedback, and insight into the startup world. Experienced founders provide one-on-one coaching and assistance. The program culminates in a demo day where founders pitch to a panel of judges, including top accelerator advisors, leading VCs, and seasoned entrepreneurs.

### Xcelerator: For Startups in the Blockchain Sectors

UC Berkeley is a leading campus for blockchain technology–based research, education, and startups.[12] The campus has an active student group called Blockchain at Berkeley, and in May 2021 a team of Berkeley students, alumni, and staff created and auctioned the first NFT based on a university's historical documents about the discovery of Nobel Prize–winning cancer immunotherapy technology.[13]

To leverage the groundswell of campus blockchain activity and invite global entrepreneurs to Berkeley's ecosystem, the Xcelerator startup program was launched in 2019 as a partnership between Berkeley's School of Business, the College of Engineering, and the Blockchain at Berkeley student group. This accelerator program provides free support for startup teams and access to resources on and off the campus. As of 2025, Xcelerator has helped eighty-

---

12. "Blockchain Degree Programs and Cryptocurrency Courses 2024," Shivam Chhuneja, May 6, 2024, https://cryptojobslist.com/blog/top-universities-blockchain-course-certification-degree.

13. All proceeds from the auction were used to support UC Berkeley blockchain research and education. For more information, see Robert Sanders, "UC Berkeley Will Auction NFTs of Nobel Prize-Winning Inventions to Fund Research," *UC Berkeley News*, May 27, 2021, https//news.berkeley.edu/2021/05/27/uc-berkeley-will-auction-nfts-of-nobel-prize-winning-inventions-to-fund-research/.

five startups that have raised more than $650 million in funding, and the program has become a pillar of the Berkeley Center for Responsible Decentralized Intelligence.

### Cyclotron Road: An Accelerator for Research Fellows

In contrast to accelerator programs that help startups launch and scale, Cyclotron Road was launched in 2014 as a research fellowship accelerator to help top technologists advance their innovations from research to commercialization.[14] Cyclotron Road is based at the Lawrence Berkeley National Lab (LBNL). The LBNL campus of buildings are located along the hillside on the eastern edge of the UC Berkeley campus. As a result of that proximity, Cyclotron Road is part of Berkeley's I&E ecosystem—as shown by many Berkeley graduate students and postdocs who have obtained Cyclotron Road fellowships.

The program recruits top innovators (not startup teams) from around the world who are at the forefront of physical science and engineering domains with promising societal benefit. Participants are required to commit full-time to the two-year fellowship. In addition to access to a range of R&D facilities, the fellowship provides entrepreneurship training and mentorship. In 2019 this research fellowship model was expanded to multiple US locations (starting with MIT Lincoln Laboratory) via a nonprofit organization called Activate. As of 2025, Cyclotron Road fellows have launched seventy-four companies, raised more than $1.85 billion in funding, hired over fourteen hundred

14. Cyclotron Road was founded by Ilan Gur, who received his PhD from UC Berkeley in materials science and engineering. Gur served as Cyclotron Road's executive director until he expanded the program across the United States as the founding CEO of Activate.org.

Lawrence Berkeley National Laboratory along the hillside on the eastern edge of the UC Berkeley campus (CREDIT: THOR SWIFT/BERKELEY LAB)

employees, and introduced innovative products across the energy, agriculture, and manufacturing industries.

### Makerspaces: Incubators for Prototyping

University makerspaces can be viewed as a category of incubator that's focused on prototyping physical stuff, instead of prototyping companies. The makerspaces at UC Berkeley are resources for campus community (as well as academic and industry affiliates) who want to design and make stuff, using advanced tools such as 3D printers, laser cutters, circuit board mills, and even advanced semiconductor fabrication tools. The campus's makerspaces provide more than just access to shared tools for the complete design process—from initial sketch to refined prototype. They also offer expert guidance, robust training, and interaction with a community of like-minded tinkerers. In many respects the makerspace communities are analogous to the cohorts of founders in Berkeley's startup accelerator programs. The makerspaces at Berkeley are listed below.

■ **The Nanolab.** The grandfather and behemoth of all prototyping spaces on the Berkeley campus is the Marvell

Nanofabrication Laboratory (known as the Nanolab) and its predecessors, the Microlab (1983–2010) and the Integrated Circuits Laboratory (1962–82). Opened in 2009, the Nanolab is a 15,000-square-foot class-100 clean room with a range of micro and nanofabrication capabilities, including lithography, etch, deposition, metrology, and packaging. As of 2025, the Nanolab has a community of academic researchers from 10 Berkeley departments and other UC campuses along with 25 highly skilled staff. The staff serves more than 70 professors, some 450 graduate and postgraduate researchers, and over 100 affiliate member companies—approximately one-quarter of which are based on Berkeley-developed technologies or founded by Berkeley alumni

- **The Invention Lab.** Opened in 2012 and located in Sutardja Dai Hall, the Invention Lab is part of CITRIS (profiled in chapter 2). The 1,700-square-foot operation cultivates the campus community's creativity by providing the training, tools, and expertise to rapidly design and prototype novel products, embedded sensing systems, and integrated mobile devices. The Invention Lab has 3D printers that are available for checkout to extend creativity and making outside of the lab, into dorm rooms and other personal workspace.

- **Jacobs Hall.** Opened in 2015, Jacobs Hall is the home of Berkeley's Jacobs Institute for Design Innovation. The building contains 24,000 square feet of design studios and maker labs (including an electronics lab, woodshop, and metal shop) with access to the latest equipment for rapid prototyping and fabrication. This facility has a Maker Pass available to faculty, students, and staff that grants semesterly access, offers safety training, and provides resources to those interested in learning more about design.

Makerspace at Jacobs Hall

- **Supernode and Cory Student Workshop.** Cory Hall in Berkeley's College of Engineering has two makerspaces. Supernode is operated by a volunteer organization and open to any member of the campus community whenever the doors are open. Cory Student Workshop has 24/7 access to a machine shop associated with Supernode.

- **b.makerspace.** Located in Moffitt Library, b.makerspace offers students from all departments the opportunity to work with new technologies like 3D printing, virtual reality, UAVs (unmanned aerial vehicles), neurotechnology, and more. There are no membership fees or user fees to access the facility. This makerspace is particularly focused on beginner makers through educational workshops.

## How a Startup Accelerator Can Drive I&E Excellence: SkyDeck

A startup accelerator is a common asset in modern university I&E ecosystems. But how can an accelerator go from just an asset to a pivotal role in the elevation of an I&E ecosystem from good to great? UC Berkeley's SkyDeck accelerator exemplifies that transformation, and its evolution is a case study in becoming one of the world's top accelerator programs.[15]

At its launch in 2012, SkyDeck had several key attributes, including (1) its location in downtown Berkeley, a block from the campus; (2) its 10,000 square feet of space on the entire top floor of what was then the tallest building in Berkeley, providing 360-degree views of the Berkeley campus, the Golden Gate Bridge, San Francisco, and the East Bay; (3) its office furnishings (including kitchen), which were left behind and donated by Intel; and (4) its connection to a large top research university— UC Berkeley.

However, the accelerator program didn't gain momentum until 2014 with the arrival of successful entrepreneur Caroline Winnett, a Berkeley Haas School of Business alumna, as its executive director. Winnett hired a talented team and together with other Berkeley colleagues, they set out to make SkyDeck a bedrock of Berkeley's I&E excellence and a leading university accelerator program.

One of the first improvements the SkyDeck team implemented was changing the (at the time) relatively unstructured program for startup teams into a structured five-and-a-half-month program. Whereas many accelerator programs are only three months long, SkyDeck's longer program (called the Berkeley Acceleration Method) enables it to expose participating teams to expert knowledge through workshops and coach-

15. Chapter 3 explores why the early concept of startup accelerators at universities was controversial and how SkyDeck was founded in 2012. Chapter 4 highlights how startup accelerators and universities can be mutually beneficial, and correspondingly why that led to the launch of several startup accelerators at Berkeley. This chapter also describes how university I&E programs such as the SkyDeck accelerator can fund their budget from outside the university.

Berkeley SkyDeck on the penthouse floor of 2150 Shattuck Avenue
(RENDERING: AD ART)

ing. The program also provides teams with more time to expand their customer discovery, pivot if necessary, achieve product-market fit, pilot go-to-market strategies, gain customer traction, hone investor pitches, and successfully raise funding. As of 2024, SkyDeck runs two cohorts annually with about twenty startup teams per cohort.

A second key enhancement that SkyDeck pursued was building a large network of experts who are enthusiastic about voluntarily advising the accelerator's startup teams. This initiative leveraged Berkeley's expansive network of alumni who have expertise in fields relevant to startups such as R&D, manufacturing, marketing, finance, law, and management. The initiative also leveraged the growing number of Berkeley faculty who are successful entrepreneurs. SkyDeck had a network of about fifty advisors in 2015, and by 2024 that network had blossomed to more than eight hundred advisors (with about two hundred of them actively involved at any given time, depending on their evolving schedules). Each startup team is carefully matched with three key advisors. Many advisors hold regular office hours (in person or online). Advisors also help SkyDeck select startup teams to join the program, and several advisors lead specialized accelerator tracks in such fields as semiconductors, biotech, climate tech, fintech, and aerospace.

SkyDeck achieved a major milestone in 2018 with the launch of SkyDeck Fund I, a $23 million (oversubscribed) seed fund led by SkyDeck advisor Chon Tang, a Berkeley EECS alumnus, entrepreneur, and investor. Expert guidance enabled the fund to avoid legal and operational conflicts with the university's nonprofit status. Even more notable, the fund contractually agreed to donate to the university 50 percent of the fund's general partner profits from its investments.[16] SkyDeck Fund II launched in 2022 with $60 million, and in 2023 the SkyDeck Opportunity Fund launched, focused on later-stage investments in the accelerator's startups. As of 2024, the SkyDeck Fund invests up to $200,000 in each startup that is accepted into the accelerator program.

SkyDeck enhanced its programs in 2021 with a rebranding of its Hotdesk incubator program, now called Pad-13. In comparison to its accelerator program, the four-month-long Pad-13 program is for founders who might only have an idea or a prototype. Pad-13 participants have access to the accelerator's workshops, advisor network, unreserved office space, and a pitch competition.

Over the years SkyDeck has expanded the eligibility of start-

---

16. The SkyDeck Fund's sharing of profits with the university was modeled in part on the structure of the Berkeley Catalyst Fund, launched in 2015.

ups that can be accepted into its program. Initially the accelerator was available only to startups with at least one member of the executive team who had an affiliation with UC Berkeley, such as alumni. That affiliation was then extended to any of the ten campuses of the University of California (e.g., UC San Francisco). Today, startups from around the world are eligible for the SkyDeck program (although there is a preference for UC-affiliated startup founders). This open eligibility contributes to Berkeley's I&E excellence by making the campus a magnet for entrepreneurship talent worldwide (in addition to being a vortex for keeping home-grown entrepreneurship talent near the campus).

Another way that SkyDeck has driven Berkeley's I&E excellence is through its series of signature events, highlighted below:

- **Demo Days.** As the culminating event of each of two annual batches of startup cohorts, SkyDeck hosts a Demo Day event that is attended by hundreds of investors. In addition to the investor pitches, the event is a celebration of the SkyDeck team, its advisors, and Berkeley's I&E exuberance.

- **Intern Fairs.** SkyDeck hosts three intern fairs each year in the spring, summer, and fall. In 2024 nearly eighteen hundred Berkeley students and more than sixty SkyDeck startups participated in the fairs, establishing some six hundred internships each year. SkyDeck also has a program that matches its startups with Berkeley postdoctoral fellows and MBA students.

- **Hackathons.** In both 2023 and 2024, SkyDeck hosted the world's largest AI-focused hackathon. More than a thousand hackers from around the world attended the thirty-six-hour, in-person events.

Caroline Winnett at SkyDeck demo day (PHOTO BY BRITTANY HOSEA-SMALL)

As of 2025, SkyDeck has become a global brand that annually receives over twenty-five hundred applications from startups and has built a vibrant community of more than eighteen hundred startups that have collectively raised over $2 billion.

## Berkeley-Affiliated Venture Capital Funds

Startup access to early-stage investors is a key resource of a robust I&E ecosystem. With its location in the San Francisco Bay Area, UC Berkeley's promising startups have had ample access to early-stage individual investors (often called angels) and venture capital firms. Berkeley amplified its access to venture capital and demonstrated the campus's trailblazing mindset by pioneering the first venture capital fund that was independent from the university but prioritized Berkeley spinouts and also shared a portion of the fund's investment profits with the campus. That model was developed by the Berkeley Catalyst Fund in 2015, emulated by the Berkeley SkyDeck Fund in 2018, and subsequently inspired several other new funds to focus on Berkeley startups and financially benefit the campus.[17] Those funds include the following (listed by formation date):

- **Berkeley Catalyst Fund.** Cofounded in 2015 by Berkeley physical chemistry PhDs Laura Smolier and Ted Hou, this fund had $24 million in capital under management and partnered with UC Berkeley's College of Chemistry and the UC Berkeley Foundation.

- **Blue Bear Ventures.** Founded in 2017 in coordination with Berkeley's CITRIS Foundry accelerator (profiled in this chapter), this fund had $3.6 million in capital under management.

- **SkyDeck Fund I.** Founded in 2018 by Berkeley EECS undergraduate alumnus Chon Tang, the fund had $24 million in capital under management and partnered with the Berkeley SkyDeck accelerator. SkyDeck Fund II launched in 2022 with $60 million in capital under management.

- **California Innovation Fund.** Founded in 2021 by Berkeley PhD and Berkeley Haas professional faculty member Kurt Beyer.

- **Berkeley Frontier Fund.** Cofounded in 2022 by a group of UC Berkeley Trustees in collaboration with the College of Engineering, this fund has $50 million in committed capital

---

17. Laura Smoliar, a cofounder and general partner of the Berkeley Catalyst Fund, led the development of the legal structure for how the fund was independent of the university, had an associated philanthropic fund, and shared a portion of its investment returns with the university. Smoliar is a UC Berkeley College of Chemistry PhD.

and is led by Berkeley alumni Richard Chan, Dylan Chiu, and Jacky Chan. The fund focuses on late-stage AI, biotech, and frontier technologies founded by Berkeley alumni. Through its investment profits, the fund supports more than thirty different organizations on campus related to entrepreneurship and innovation.

- **BEVC.** Cofounded in 2024 by Berkeley undergraduate alumna Widya Mulyasasmita and UC San Francisco postdoctoral fellow Rowan Chapman, the fund has more than $50 million in capital under management and was launched in coordination with QB3.

In addition to the above venture capital funds, the following two venture capital firms have had a formative influence on Berkeley's I&E ecosystem:

- **Osage University Partners.** OUP was founded in 2010 based on the unique strategy of building a network of universities that transfer to OUP the universities' unused rights to participate in future investment rounds of startups that obtain intellectual property licenses from those universities. In return, OUP shares its investment profits and industry knowledge with its university network. As of 2024, OUP had raised four funds totaling more than $800 million in capital under management.

- **The House.** Founded in 2015 by two Berkeley undergraduate alumni, Jeremy Fiance and Cameron Baradar, initially The House operated an accelerator program as well as an early-stage investment fund. While The House prioritizes Berkeley startups, it doesn't share a portion of its investment profits with the campus. As of 2024, The House had raised three funds totaling $330 million in capital under management. The VC firm's first fund in 2015 was $6 million, its second fund in 2019 was $44 million, and its third fund in 2023 was $115 million.[18]

The Berkeley campus also has a variety of small funds that target very early-stage student startups. These funds include the following:

- **Haas Impact Fund.** This fund invests in early-stage impact-oriented startups. The Student Venture Partners lead sourcing, diligence, and portfolio stewardship of the companies. The Student Venture Partners pitch recommendations to a panel of judges for up to $75,000 in equity investments from the Haas Impact Fund along with potential additional funding from a select group of funds.

- **Sega Sammy Fund for New Media.** This fund provides $5,000 in awards to four student startups annually that are focused on such ventures as entertainment, gaming, or new technology.[19]

- **Trione Student Venture Fund.** This fund provides a prize package that includes $5,000 to enable experiential learning to twenty early-stage student startups each year.[20]

Many other early-stage investors have funded Berkeley spinouts, including well-known venture capital firms, individual

18. Kyle Wiggers, "The House Fund Aims to Invest a Fresh $115M in Berkeley-affiliated Startups," *Tech Crunch*, October 25, 2023, https://techcrunch.com/2023/10/25/the-house-fund-aims-to-invest-a-fresh-115m-in-berkeley-affiliated-startups/.

19. The Sega Sammy Fund was made possible by philanthropic funding from Sega Sammy.

20. The Trione Student Venture Fund was made possible by philanthropic funding from UC Berkeley MBA alumnus Victor Trione.

angel investors (many of whom are Berkeley alumni), and networks of alumni investors, such as the Berkeley Angel Network and Strawberry Creek Ventures. Additionally, the student group Berkeley Venture Capital was launched in 2021 to provide students with hands-on experience in sourcing and screening startups through the entire VC deal flow process. The organization provides real-world experience by pairing students with experienced VCs.

## Bringing Together I&E Leaders: Berkeley Innovation Council

By 2014 the entrepreneurship exuberance at UC Berkeley, combined with its decentralized management, fueled a boom in new I&E programs and initiatives across multiple departments, schools, and colleges. The campus's I&E ecosystem was quickly broadening and deepening in impressive, productive, and autonomous ways. However, campus leadership came to the realization that Berkeley wasn't achieving its full I&E potential because (1) I&E activities were uncoordinated, overlapping, and inefficiently using campus resources; and (2) students and non–UC Berkeley people who were capable of and interested in leveraging Berkeley's I&E resources were confused by how to navigate the ecosystem.

In 2015 that situation led the campus's vice chancellor for research to "knit our I&E ecosystem together" by establishing the Berkeley Innovation Council made up of faculty, staff, students, and recent alumni who had leadership roles in the campus's I&E ecosystem. Initially about forty people were invited to attend the council's biweekly one-hour brown bag lunch meetings. During its first year the council had four I&E subgroups focused on coordinating and maximizing I&E infrastructure, curriculum, mentors/alumni, and stories (for marketing purposes).

By 2019 about eighty people were on the council, and the campus's new chief innovation and entrepreneurship officer (CIEO) took over chairing the council. Most agendas for the monthly meeting included newsworthy updates from the CIEO and council members as well as a "master class" on an I&E topic apropos to the council.

## Online Portal to Berkeley's I&E Ecosystem: begin.berkeley.edu

By 2014, UC Berkeley's surging I&E ecosystem had become confusing to many people, including Berkeley students and early-stage investors. One obvious way to decrease that problem was to create an online portal that would help people learn about and leverage the campus's I&E resources.

To address this issue, in 2015 staff from Berkeley's Office of Intellectual Property and Research Alliances as well as from the office of the vice chancellor for research came together to develop a website with a directory of the ecosystem's resources and a one-on-one concierge service to guide individuals through the ecosystem. The website's home page featured a clickable infographic in the shape of a pentagon that depicted Berkeley's I&E ecosystem.

Typical of the exuberant and decentralized nature of Berkeley's I&E ecosystem, several other departments and individuals also posted online directories of the campus's I&E ecosystem. One of the challenges of making these online portals useful was not only providing a comprehensive snapshot of the vast ecosystem but also keeping the directories up to date with all the dynamism in the ecosystem. That maintenance required on-

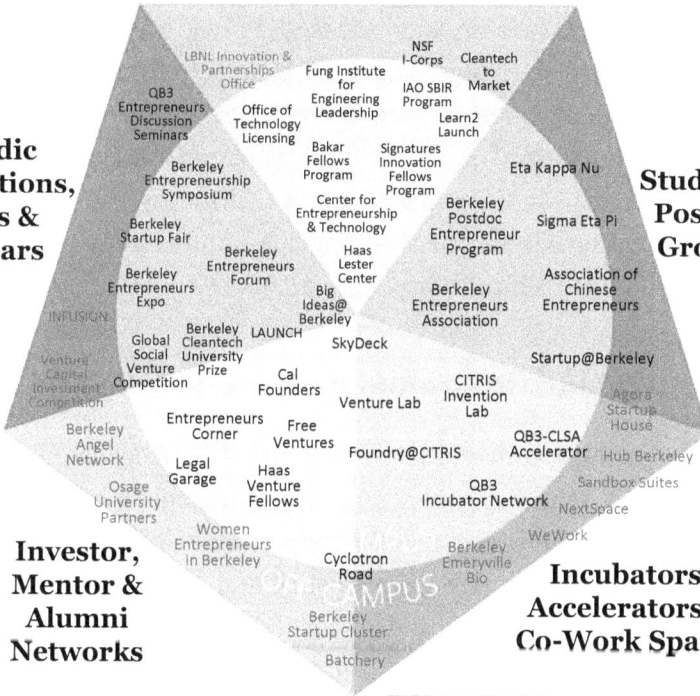

An early version of an infographic for Berkeley's I&E ecosystem (CREATED BY MIKE ALVAREZ COHEN IN BERKELEY'S OFFICE OF TECHNOLOGY LICENSING)

going staff diligence and associated funding. In 2017 the State of California government distributed $2.2 million in funding to each of the ten University of California campuses for onetime expenditures to "expand or accelerate economic development in the state in ways that are aligned with other efforts to support innovation and entrepreneurship."[21]

21. California State Legislature, Assembly Bill 2664, "University of California: Innovation and Entrepreneurship Expansion," https://legiscan.com/CA/text/AB2664/2015.

Berkeley used a portion of that funding to develop a more sophisticated version of its I&E ecosystem online portal. In May 2017 the new version was released as begin.berkeley.edu. Stephen Rice in Berkeley's Office of Intellectual Property and Industry Research Alliances coined "Begin as the Berkeley Gateway to Innovation." As of 2018, the website's upgrades have been led by Keith McAleer in Berkeley's SCET program. As of 2025, Begin has undergone several upgrades and is a key platform for Berkeley's I&E community.

## Funding I&E Programs: Innovation Services

As with most universities, education and research are at the core of UC Berkeley's mission, and accordingly they are a higher priority for the campus's budget in comparison to Berkeley activities that support entrepreneurs and their startups. Consequently, the campus's funding for I&E programs has often been limited in amount and duration. Not surprisingly, charging entrepreneurs and startups is not a solution because whatever funds they have are focused on building their companies. This situation has compelled many Berkeley I&E programs to pursue self-sustaining financial models from sources outside of the university, such as large corporations, government agencies, and other educational institutions.

To address this funding challenge for Berkeley's I&E ecosystem, in 2014 the campus's Industry Alliances Office (IAO) began developing expertise in agreements in which a third party funds a Berkeley I&E program. By 2019 the IAO had honed this capability and formalized it as a Berkeley I&E platform called Innovation Services.[22] The platform systematically helps campus I&E

22. As of 2024, the Innovation Services platform has been led by Eric

programs design external funding models, pursue third-party sponsors, as well as draft and negotiate agreements. As of 2024, the Innovation Services platform has implemented the following five categories of programs:

- **Accelerator Programs for Startup Teams.** This agreement category enables third-party entities to select and sponsor startup teams to participate in a Berkeley accelerator program. Typically the sponsoring entities are non-US universities and government agencies.

  The IAO first developed this Innovation Services category in 2014 for SkyDeck's Innovation Partners Program. The program enables startups to participate in SkyDeck programming with sponsorship from another entity, such as a government economic development office. The program's fees have been a key contributor to SkyDeck's budget. In 2021 the IAO developed a variation of this category for the Berkeley-Taiwan Health Innovator Accelerator. Under this agreement the National Development Council in Taiwan sends Taiwan startups to an accelerator program operated by Berkeley's School of Public Health.

- **Educational Programs for Entrepreneurship Students.** In contrast to sponsoring startup teams, this agreement category enables third-party entities to select and sponsor students to participate in a Berkeley entrepreneurship education program. The sponsors are typically non-US universities.

  The IAO first developed this Innovation Services category in 2015 for SCET's Global Partners Program. The program

---

Giegrich, the director of the IAO and has substantial support from UC Berkeley's legal team and other staff in the Office of Intellectual Property and Industry Research Alliances.

enables students to come to Berkeley to attend SCET's courses and events as well as access other Berkeley I&E resources. As of 2024, more than twelve universities have participated in the Global Partners Program.

▪ **Innovation Programs for Visiting Delegations.** This agreement enables delegations to visit the campus to attend a series of events consisting of research seminars, startup presentations, and other activities that are all focused on cutting-edge topics such as AI, health, or climate. The sponsors are typically non-US governments. The delegations are often a mix of government officials, private sector leaders, and university representatives.

The IAO first developed this Innovation Services category in 2023 for the CITRIS Hub's blitz of activities called Innovation Intensives. In addition to activities based at Berkeley, Innovation Intensives can include tours of the other three University of California campuses (Davis, Merced, and Santa Cruz) that are part of CITRIS to meet with their researchers and startups.

▪ **I&E Support for Third-Party Programs.** Sometimes a third-party I&E funding partner wants to bring a Berkeley I&E program to the partner's region, instead of sending their entrepreneurs or startups to Berkeley. For those opportunities this agreement category enables campus I&E programs to deploy support services to entities that are located far from the Berkeley campus. These agreements are intentionally structured as support services, not as Berkeley I&E branch locations because that would require a long approval process by the university's regents. However, to help leverage Berkeley's I&E brand and promote the distant I&E

programs, the university can provide a revenue-generating trademark license of a Berkeley I&E brand.

The IAO first developed this Innovation Services category in 2022 for SkyDeck as part of the Berkeley SkyDeck Europe, Milano accelerator program. That accelerator is located in Milano's innovation district and funded by the Lendlease Corporation and Cariplo Factory. The arrangement includes the licensing of the Berkeley SkyDeck trademark.

■ **Startup Services for Industry Affiliate Research Programs.** Many universities have industry affiliate research programs in which multiple companies in a market sector (e.g., semiconductors, microelectromechanical systems, or AI) pay the university membership fees to collaborate on precompetitive research. This Innovation Services agreement category enables Berkeley's industry affiliate research programs to offer startup accelerator services to the program's members that are startups.

The agreement category is especially suitable to industry affiliate programs in market sectors that are conducive to successful startups. So it's not surprising that the IAO first developed this category in 2022 for the Berkeley AI Research (BAIR) industry affiliate program. Under this program BAIR provides accelerator programming for its members that are startups. Moreover, its startup members can pay for BAIR's annual membership in the form of stock equity instead of cash.

Berkeley's Innovation Services platform has achieved its success by balancing the oftentimes opposing goals of innovating on new types of university agreements but safeguarding the university from undue risks—especially those caused by activities that drift from the institution's core mission. Achieving this balance is exacerbated by the pressure on the university's large bureaucratic organization to make decisions at the speed and agility required by entrepreneurs, startups, and the market. The key success factors include:

- Developing university staff to have a culture to innovate but also the judgment and competency to manage risks.

- Piloting novel programs to mitigate their risks during the process of testing, refining, and either expanding or ending them.

- Converting novel agreements into platforms by templating and extrapolating their core elements so that they can be applied to multiple, similar campus programs.

## Leveraging the Law School Community: Startup@BerkeleyLaw

With its location across the bay from San Francisco and about fifty miles north of the heart of Silicon Valley, it's not surprising that many students at UC Berkeley's law school are interested in working with startups while pursuing their legal education on campus and during their careers after graduating. That student interest led to the 2015 launch of Startup@BerkeleyLaw, a collaboration between the law school's Berkeley Center for Law and Business and the Berkeley Center for Law and Technology.[23] The collaboration's programs train Berkeley Law students to help startups succeed, guide new business ventures through their

23. Startup@BerkeleyLaw was made possible by philanthropic funding from the law firm Wilson Sonsini Goodrich & Rosati.

legal issues, and offer entrepreneurs access to legal experts, courses, and workshops. As of 2024, the collaboration has the following three signature programs:

### FORM+FUND

FORM+FUND is Berkeley Law's free workshop series for Berkeley-affiliated entrepreneurs. The workshop teaches the core legal, financial, and organizational aspects of starting and scaling a venture-backed company. Sessions are taught by leading Silicon Valley attorneys, entrepreneurs, and venture capitalists. FORM+FUND Fellows schedule office hours to provide gratis guidance to workshop participants.

### The Startup Law Initiative

The Startup Law Initiative provides free legal incorporation services to low-income and diverse startup founders and local entrepreneurs. These services are provided by Berkeley law students under the supervision of experienced attorneys. Students are put into small groups and assigned a startup client to work with over the course of a year. In the fall semester students help the clients incorporate and thereby gain experience in client intake, drafting and filing documents (e.g., articles of incorporation), as well as interacting with clients and supervising attorneys. In the spring semester students work on a variety of documents, including template forms commonly used by early-stage companies. In addition to all that experiential learning, students attend workshops to learn legal, financial, and organizational aspects of starting and scaling a company. Each semester a group of students create and present a workshop on startup law basics to Berkeley's entrepreneurship community.

### Berkeley IP Practicum

Patenting an invention is just one step for startups in progressing their technology toward commercialization. Startups also need to ensure that they aren't infringing on existing patents that could limit a startup's ability to commercialize its technology. Ensuring that a startup's intellectual property landscape is free of obstacles (known as "freedom to operate") can be crucial to a startup's ability to attract investment. However, this freedom-to-operate analysis can take many hours of a patent attorney's time and consequently can be expensive. To bridge this gap for early-stage startups, the Law School offers the Berkeley IP Practicum, in which selected startups work with a team of law students with technical backgrounds and an experienced attorney to perform an IP landscape or freedom-to-operate analysis.

## Enabling Startups to Perform New Product R&D in Faculty Labs

From time to time, UC Berkeley–affiliated startups have wanted to use unique R&D capabilities in some faculty labs to conduct early-stage commercial R&D, especially if reproducing those R&D capabilities would cost the startup tens or hundreds of thousands of dollars. Likewise, many Berkeley faculty have been willing to temporarily allow this promising early-stage new product R&D.

However, the university didn't have a way to address the many issues associated with allowing commercial R&D in faculty labs, such as (1) maintaining oversight of how campus facilities are used; (2) prioritizing research and education over commercial use; (3) ensuring environmental, health, and safety compliance; (4) monitoring private use to stay within the safe harbor under the nonprofit tax code; (5) managing conflicts of interest; (6) clarifying intellectual property ownership; (7) establishing fair market value fees; (8) maintaining best practices for campus visitors including insurance and secure facilities, as well as (9) addressing private gain issues, and (10) potential public perceptions of misuse.

In early 2017, Cyclotron Road, the research accelerator at the Lawrence Berkeley National Lab, expressed interest in expanding from the national lab to the adjacent Berkeley campus. The Berkeley vice chancellor for research also wanted to explore that opportunity. As a result, the Berkeley Office of Intellectual Property & Industry Research Alliances (IPIRA) launched an initiative to develop a program that would enable startups affiliated with Cyclotron Road (and the other startup accelerators in Berkeley's I&E ecosystem) to temporarily use faculty labs for new product R&D in ways that would address all the issues.[24] IPIRA developed a program that leveraged three existing Berkeley programs: the core user facility program (which allows commercial R&D users), the visiting industrial fellow program (which allows non-UC employees to conduct research on the Berkeley campus), and the visiting scholars program.

Allowing visitors to conduct commercial R&D in a faculty lab, albeit under lots of university oversight and limitations, is radical. Few, if any, other universities officially offer this capability. Nonetheless, in July 2017 the Research Policy, Analysis and

*(continued on page 134)*

---

24. The Cyclotron Road director who instigated this program was Ilan Gurr. The vice chancellor for research who catalyzed the program was Paul Alivisatos. The subsequent vice chancellor for research who approved the program was Randy Katz. The person in the Office of Intellectual Property and Industry Research Alliance who architected the program was Mike Alvarez Cohen. Lynn Hollyer in the Industry Alliances Program helped Cohen implement the program.

# Chirp Microsystems: A University, Industry, Government, Spouse Collaboration

In 2018 the Tokyo-based electronics giant TDK Corporation acquired the UC Berkeley startup Chirp Microsystems, enabling the Berkeley-based company's fifteen employees to scale up its ultrasonic sensor technology for a wide range of applications.

That acquisition highlighted the story of a husband and wife cofounding duo. It was also exemplary of how a National Science Foundation Industry/University Cooperative Research Center (I/UCRC) helped create an industry sector, an innovative technology, and a successful startup. The I/UCRC is called the Berkeley Sensor and Actuator Center (BSAC). It was organized in 1986 to develop a science, engineering, and technology base for microsensors, microactuators, and microelectromechanical systems (MEMS).[a]

The story of Chirp starts in 2012 with the invention of a MEMS ultrasonic sensor by a team of BSAC researchers that included UC Davis mechanical engineering professor David Horsely. Horsely received his BS, MS, and PhD in mechanical

Chirp Microsystems team (SOURCE: CHIRP)

engineering from Berkeley. He had held several R&D positions in industry before joining in 2003 the Department of Mechanical and Aerospace Engineering at UC Davis, about sixty miles east of Berkeley. BSAC expanded to include the Davis campus in 1998, and Horsley became a BSAC faculty co-director in 2004. The BSAC research that led to the ultrasonic invention was funded by DARPA and Analog Devices, Inc., which was a BSAC corporate member.

To commercialize the ultrasonic sensor, Horsley cofounded Chirp Microsystems with his spouse, Michelle Kiang. Kiang was the company's CEO and Horsley its CTO. Kiang received her MS and PhD degrees in electrical engineering from Berkeley, where the couple had met. Before Chirp, Kiang had a career in industry, including cofounding two hard tech startups with successful exits.

Chirp licensed the ultrasonic sensor's patent rights from the university, and in addition to BSAC, the startup leveraged several other Berkeley I&E resources, such as the SkyDeck startup ac-

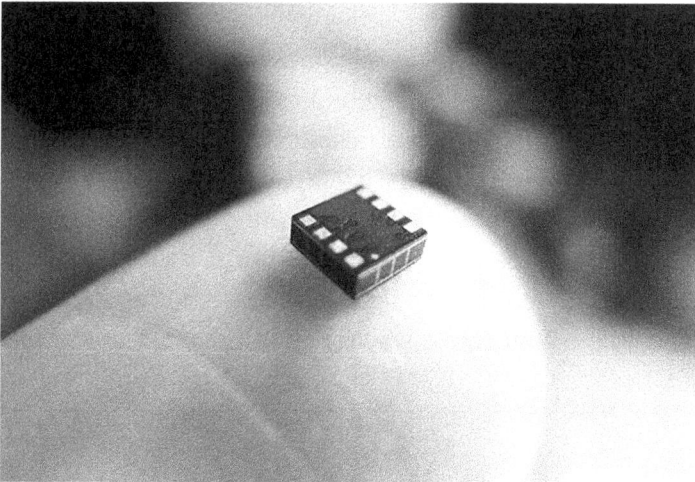

Chirp Ultrasonic ToF sensor, integrated with a signal processing ASIC
(SOURCE: CHIRP)

celerator (profiled in chapter 3 as well as this chapter), and the campus's Marvell Nanofabrication shared R&D laboratory (highlighted in this chapter). Horsely and the team used the Marvell "NanoLab" to produce prototypes of the company's sensors for demonstrations to potential customers and investors.

Chirp raised $3.2 million in 2015 in a seed round of financing with institutional investors, and in 2017 the company raised another $1.5 million. That year Chirp launched its first product, a millimeter-size, ultra-low power, single-chip sensor that functions like sonar or echolocation, sending ultrasonic sound waves and then measuring how long it takes for the returning echo. The product enables precise sensing, ranging from several centimeters to several meters. It has many applications—for example, it can enable users to interact with a device without touching the device or even interact with a device that doesn't have a screen (such as a wristband or ring). In comparison to alternative sensor technologies, such as IR sensors, Chirp's ultrasonic sensor is more compact, less costly, requires less power, and works under any lighting conditions, including direct sunlight.

In a 2018 interview with *EE Times*, Kiang said, "Of course, we founded Chirp, not to sell, but to grow our own business. But last fall, when we were raising money for our series A—which was oversubscribed—we also heard of TDK's interest." She added, "We were open to the idea of becoming a part of a larger organization because the opportunity appears to give us the chance to live in the same ecosystem they are already in, and it could become a way for us to scale our business at a much faster pace."[b]

One of the interesting aspects of the Chirp story is the success of the husband and wife cofounding duo. "It worked well for us," Kiang remarked. "Dave is the leading expert in his field and also experienced in managing technical teams. Whereas I brought the business experience from founding and running two hard tech startups prior to Chirp as well as working at large companies in corporate development and strategy." She added, "We have complementary skills and deep respect for one another. We'd worked together prior to Chirp, first at the company we both joined right after graduating from Berkeley, and then at my first startup, where Dave led the system engineering team. So we knew we could work well together. Also, we felt fortunate that we could spend more time together than a typical couple with separate careers."

However, Kiang also observed some not-so-positive aspects. "The flip side of the advantages was that there was little separation between family and work time, meaning we were constantly talking shop even at home (and our daughter can attest to that). Finally, we had to deal with certain negative perceptions that some investors had about a husband and wife team, especially when the wife is the CEO (not the CFO or something like that). In any case, we are happy to be in good company with the likes of Marvell and VMWare husband and wife cofounders." ▪

a. "Chirp Slurped up by TDK," *EE Times*, February 28, 2018, www.eetimes.com/chirp-slurped-up-by-tdk.

b. BSAC researchers at UC Berkeley developed other MEMS technology that led to the successful startups Berkeley Lights (profiled in chapter 3), Iota Biosciences (profiled in chapter 5), Discera, and Silicon Clocks.

Coordination team in the University of California Office of the President approved a two-year pilot of the novel program. The pilot was named the Shared Special User Facility for Innovation & Entrepreneurship (SSUFIE) program. In July 2019, IPIRA completed a review report of the SSUFIE pilot, and the vice chancellor for research agreed to continue the program.

In 2022 the SSUFIE program was brought under the Berkeley Research Infrastructure Commons (RIC) program (profiled in chapter 5) and renamed the RIC FLEXIE program (Faculty Lab eXceptional-use for Innovation & Entrepreneurship). As of 2024, more than two dozen startups have leveraged the FLEXIE program, including notable spinouts such as Iota Biosciences (which was acquired by Astellas Pharma in 2020 for approximately $300 million).

## EVCP Manifesto Dinners

*September 23, 2016 email to a group of faculty and staff from Paul Alivisatos, UC Berkeley's Executive Vice Chancellor and Provost:*

As you know, there have been many successful new ventures formed by our students and faculty, and successful incubators established, on or near campus, including Skydeck (at 2150 Shattuck). Entrepreneurship has captured the imagination of many of our students and particularly those in STEM and in business and law. Berkeley attracts many top undergraduate and graduate students who have one eye on the entrepreneurial opportunities in the Bay Area.

I am writing to invite you to participate in a process which is very important to the future of the campus—refining our strategy with respect to the campus involvement in, and support of, faculty and student engagement with entrepreneurship initiatives.

Despite some campus support, and our many startup successes, Berkeley is not perceived by some as being as supportive as MIT or Stanford and some other peers we respect. This may not in fact be the case, but it is a perspective that some faculty, students, alumni, and industry partners (or would-be partners) have come to hold. Some believe that creative activity, entrepreneurship, and applying our research is not a fully endorsed activity. Perhaps campus leadership needs to articulate its position more clearly?

I have decided, in consultation with some of our faculty, donors, and other constituents that it would be helpful if we could clarify and articulate our strategy and our commitment to seeing greater impact from campus research and creative activity. To that end, I would like to host a series of dinners between now and the end of the calendar year to solicit your input on these issues. David Teece from the Institute for Business Innovation (and a noted scholar on innovation) believes that it would be valuable if many of us could come together around a manifesto on campus research, innovation, and entrepreneurship, stating how faculty involved and/or close to such activities see the affirmative case while simultaneously recognizing issues to which some constituents are sensitive. He has provided a discussion paper (attached) and is willing to lead the discussion at the first dinner.

The Teece paper suggests a need for (1) more innovative and entrepreneurial activity, stronger and deeper communications, and engagement with outside organizations; and (2) a stronger commitment to fundamental and applied research focused on generating "enabling" or "anchoring" technologies that will help solve medium and longer term societal problems. If properly executed, he believes this strategy can help renew and enhance the Berkeley brand and the campus endowment and expand the utility and impact of campus research. Teece also believes that a more proactive stance would help preserve campus independence and sustain its unfettered, truth seeking (and conventional wisdom shattering) academic environment.

I believe this initiative is important to our campus and I do hope you can join the manifesto dinners.

# FIVE

# Harmonizing and Leveraging the Juggernaut

Imagination is not only the uniquely human capacity to envision that which is not, and therefore the fount of all invention and innovation. In its arguably most transformative and revelatory capacity, it is the power that enables us to empathize with humans whose experiences we have never shared.

—■ J. K. ROWLING

## Berkeley I&E, 2019–2024

UC Berkeley's I&E juggernaut fundamentally changed in 2019 with the appointment of Professor Richard Lyons as the campus's inaugural chief information and entrepreneurship officer (CIEO). Berkeley's sprawling, decentralized I&E ecosystem finally had a leader. While not wanting to dampen the ecosystem's vibrancy, the CIEO pursued an ambitious agenda that included raising the worldwide visibility of Berkeley's I&E excellence and harmonizing the ecosystem's activities—all while expanding I&E capacity and broadening its benefits across the campus community.

Soon after the CIEO's appointment, the stature and momentum for innovation and entrepreneurship at Berkeley skyrocketed with the announcement that I&E had become one of the prioritized multidisciplinary tracks of the campus's $7.3 billion Light the Way philanthropic capital campaign. That emphasis catalyzed increasing amounts of philanthropy focused on Berkeley I&E—for example, donations to fund the Life Sciences Entrepreneurship Center (profiled in this chapter), the Bakar Labs (profiled in chapter 6), and an initiative to raise the visibility of Berkeley's I&E accomplishments called Project Tipping Point (highlighted in this chapter).

Among the first outcomes of the CIEO's agenda was the 2020 launch of the campus-wide certificate program Berkeley Changemaker (profiled in this chapter). This curriculum leveraged Berkeley's I&E excellence by expanding the mindset of entrepreneurship beyond starting commercial ventures to also pursuing new, risky, and meaningful endeavors across all aspects of a person's career and life.

In an analogous effort, this time to increase a funding stream for the campus, the CIEO team launched the Equity Solutions Services team (profiled in this chapter) in 2021. The group's charter was to expand and diversify Berkeley's contractual agreements that support the university's mission and that would result in the university owning stock equity in startups (with the expectation that some of that startup equity would eventually provide out sized financial returns to the campus).

Five years after its conception (which was before the creation of the CIEO role), another I&E game-changer for Berkeley launched with the 2022 opening of Bakar Labs and its incubator building, the Bakar BioEnginuity Hub (profiled in this chapter).[1] With more than 40,000 square feet of shared laboratory space,

---

1. The Bakar BioEnginuity Hub and Bakar Labs were made possible by philanthropic funding from the Bakar Foundation.

the hub included associated entrepreneurship programs for dozens of life sciences startups.

In anticipation of the Bakar Labs's opening, the CIEO team launched the Life Sciences Entrepreneurship Center (profiled in this chapter) to build on Berkeley's many programs for life sciences innovators.[2] These include the Innovative Genomics Institute (founded by Berkeley professor and Nobel laureate Jennifer Doudna), the California Institute for Quantitative Biosciences (QB3), and the Bio Track of the Berkeley SkyDeck startup accelerator.

In 2024, five years after taking the reins as the first leader of Berkeley's I&E ecosystem, Lyons was appointed as Berkeley's chancellor. That announcement not only marked a capstone of this phase of Berkeley's I&E ascendance, it was also emblematic of how I&E had become core to the campus's ethos and future.

## Leading Without Authority: Chief Innovation and Entrepreneurship Officer

On July 10, 2019, UC Berkeley announced Professor Richard Lyons as the campus's first chief innovation and entrepreneurship officer (CIEO). Lyons had served as dean of Berkeley's Haas School of Business and was a cofounder and board member of SkyDeck. The inaugural CIEO's role was to work with campus partners to further develop and communicate Berkeley's rich portfolio of I&E activities to the benefit of the campus's students, faculty, staff, and startups as well as, importantly, to con-

2. The Life Sciences Entrepreneurship Center was made possible by philanthropic funding from UC Berkeley alumni Mark and Stephanie Robinson as well as from alumnus and adjunct professor David Kirn and his wife, Kristin Ahlquist.

nect those activities so that they add up to more than the sum of their parts. The position was also responsible for developing strategies to raise the visibility of Berkeley's I&E activities internally and externally and to create high-value partnerships with stakeholders. During his interview for the CIEO position, Lyons said, "If together we can improve the transformation of Berkeley's prodigious intellectual product, across the whole campus, into greater societal benefit, then we will have achieved a great deal."[3]

The CIEO position at Berkeley is challenging because the campus's numerous I&E programs are decentrally managed across a range of units, including the College of Engineering, School of Business, Law School, QB3, CITRIS, and the office of the vice chancellor for research. The CIEO reports to the vice chancellor for research (VCR) and accordingly the VCR's I&E programs were consolidated under Lyons. Those programs included the intellectual property licensing office (profiled in chapter 2) and the SkyDeck accelerator (profiled in chapters 3 and 4). Also, Lyons replaced the VCR as the chair of Berkeley's ninety-person I&E Council (profiled in chapter 4).

Still, Lyons's ability to harmonize all the I&E programs while lacking formal control over most of them required skilled advocacy, communication, and relationship-building. The COVID-19 pandemic's shutdown of in-person activity only a few months after Lyons officially started in his CIEO role was another challenge he and the Berkeley I&E community had to overcome. To pursue the CIEO's objective, Lyons assembled a team composed

3. "Former Haas Dean Named New Campus Innovation Officer," *UC Berkeley Research*, July 10, 2019, https://vcresearch.berkeley.edu/news/former-haas-dean-named-new-campus-innovation-officer.

of Laura Paxton Hassner (a member of Berkeley's professional faculty) as his strategic advisor, Berkeley student interns, and members of the campus's I&E community.

A strategy that Lyons and his team used to synergistically build I&E capacity without centralized authority was structuring new I&E programs as platforms that enable different units on the campus (at their own discretion) to plug into and leverage.[4] Elevating a program into a platform is achieved by abstracting a program's assets into templates that can be flexibly applied to multiple areas of the campus and then communicating the benefits of using the platform across the campus. In addition to increasing capacity, the platform approach also harmonizes different programs throughout the ecosystem.[5]

One example of a platform that the CIEO team launched in 2021 was Berkeley's Research Infrastructure Commons (profiled in this chapter). Under that platform shared R&D facilities across the campus can decide (they aren't forced) to join the commons (known as the RIC) and thereby leverage its documents and processes that make it easy for users—particularly commercial users who pay nonsubsidized commercial rates—to share R&D facilities and thereby financially support the maintenance and expansion of those facilities.

To raise the national and global visibility of Berkeley's I&E success, the CIEO team assembled a steering committee and ad-

---

4. Examples of well-known platforms include Apple iTunes for playing a variety of audio and video content, Microsoft Windows for running a variety of computer applications, and Wikipedia for crowdsourcing a variety of information.

5. For more information on UC Berkeley's I&E platforms, see "A Platforms Vision for Advancing University Innovation," April 24, 2024, iande.berkeley.edu/sites/default/files/4_24_platforms_that_advance_ie_at_ucb.pdf.

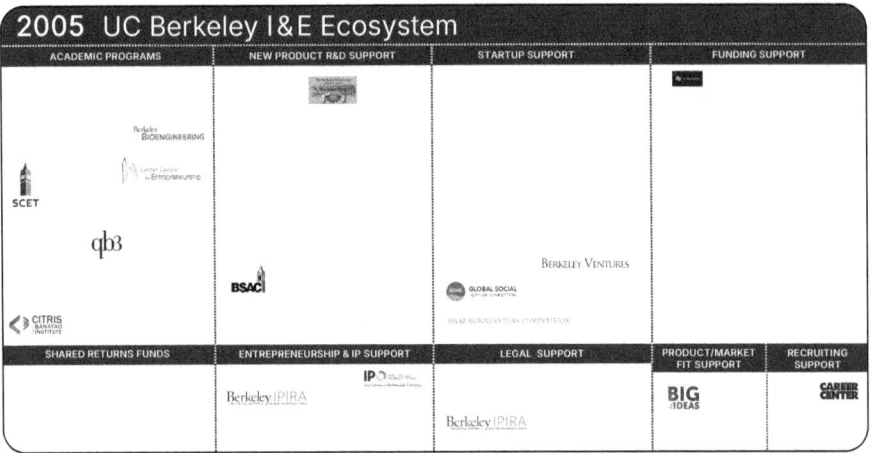

2005 UC Berkeley I&E Ecosystem

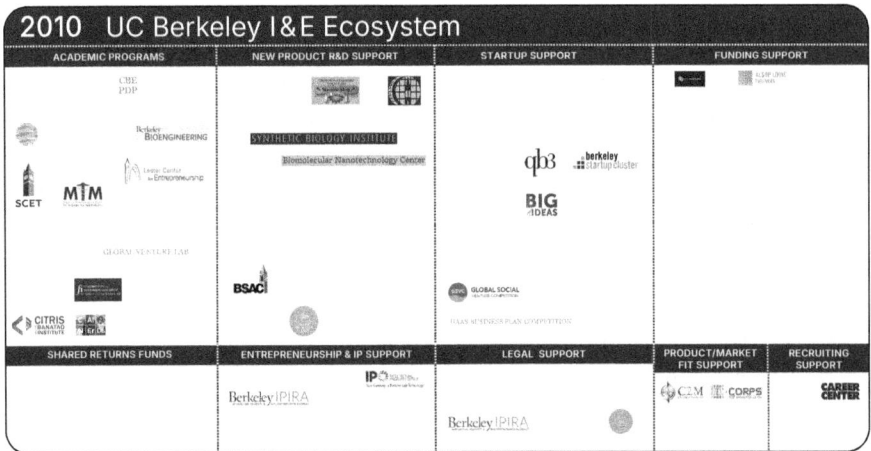

2010 UC Berkeley I&E Ecosystem

visory group. Called Project Tipping Point, this initiative leveraged a variety of communications-related materials, including
pulse survey results, a presentation about the growth of Berkeley's I&E ecosystem using visual snapshots of I&E programs in
2005, 2010, 2015, and 2025, and a list of the top one hundred
Berkeley faculty founders. This invest-in-visibility effort was en-

2015 UC Berkeley I&E Ecosystem

2025 UC Berkeley I&E Ecosystem

abled by philanthropy dedicated to telling Berkeley's I&E story more powerfully externally.[6]

The I&E team launched another platform, Equity Solutions

---

6. Project Tipping Point was made possible by philanthropic funding from UC Berkeley alumnus Matthew Levin.

Services (profiled in this chapter), to harmonize all the Berkeley-affiliated venture capital funds, improve the management of Berkeley's stock equity holdings and investment rights in startup companies, and explore new opportunities to benefit from the technology and startups that Berkeley produces.

To synergize and build on the several I&E programs focused on life sciences technology, entrepreneurship, and startups, the CIEO team launched the Life Sciences Entrepreneurship Center (profiled in this chapter).

In 2023, four years after the first CIEO started, PitchBook ranked Berkeley as the number one university for undergraduate alumni who founded venture capital–backed startups. In response to that ranking, Lyons has joked that "correlation doesn't imply causation." Nonetheless, by 2024 the sense that Berkeley was underperforming in its I&E outcomes had been practically eliminated. However, there were still opportunities for improvement in the next phases of Berkeley's growth.

## Broadening the Entrepreneurship Mindset: Berkeley Changemaker

By 2019, UC Berkeley's surge in I&E activity had become exhilarating to select segments of the campus (mostly in the STEM fields) in which education and research are conducive to startups. However, that success threatened to create a cultural rift with large segments of the campus (mostly the humanities and social sciences) that aren't conventional pathways for entrepreneurs and startups. Indeed, the 2018 report on *Entrepreneurship at UC Berkeley* states: "[M]any Cal students (especially those outside engineering and business disciplines) seem to have an arms-length attitude to entrepreneurship—'It isn't for me'—and do not venture into Berkeley's entrepreneurial ecosystem."

Allowing this nascent rift in the campus community to fester could have been especially problematic for Berkeley because of its comprehensive breadth of academic disciplines. So the report went on to state: "We [This report's authors] encourage campus to promote an inclusive view of entrepreneurship: from founders, to early employees in new ventures, to those who take personal career 'risks' to work on worthy causes that could include starting nonprofits and social impact organizations." That recommendation inspired Berkeley's executive leadership to turn the potential problem into an opportunity to expand the benefits of entrepreneurship across the campus by going all in on a broader definition of entrepreneurship.

In 2020 that strategy galvanized the campus to launch the Berkeley Changemaker, a campus-wide certificate program that includes a robust curriculum of more than forty academically rigorous courses in departments across the campus, based on three throughlines: critical thinking, communication, and collaboration. The curriculum activates undergraduates' passions and develops a sharper sense of who they want to be and how to make that happen. Those with an agency for making our world better have been drawn to this expansive definition and narrative of entrepreneurship.

In structuring the Changemaker curriculum, the program's founding leadership team composed of Alex Budak, Laura Paxton Hassner, and Jay Stowsky had to contend with assuring "academic heft," managing the dual goal posts of "social impact" and "commercial impact," and eliminating any impression that "changemaker" is merely a euphemism for "entrepreneurship." To address those challenges, all the program's courses and workshops include a clear and consistent focus on the core pillars of critical thinking, communication, and collaboration. These are central to a great education and changemaking, regardless of

(continued on page 150)

# Iota Biosciences: Neural Dust for Bioelectronic Implantable Medical Devices

The spinout story of Iota Biosciences started in 2012 with a collaboration between UC Berkeley EECS professors Jose Carmena and Michel Maharbiz, a self-described gadget builder.[a] Inspired by advances in electronics miniaturization, manufacturing, and power efficiency, the researchers teamed up to improve microelectrode-based devices that could be used to monitor and stimulate nerve, muscle, and organ tissue. At that time the tiny electrodes needed to be wired to a larger device to provide power, control, and communication functionality. That limited their potential as medical implants.

"The idea at first was to have free-floating motes in the brain with RF powering them," Carmena said. But they encountered a fundamental problem. The long wavelength of RF signals requires an antenna that is too large for a long-term implantable device. "There was a meeting at which everything died, because we were like two orders of magnitude away from

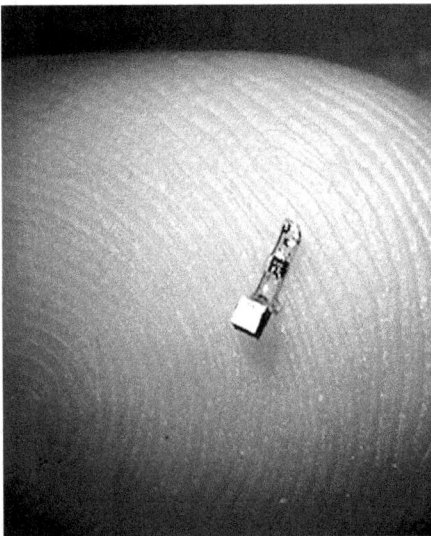

This micron-sensor implant measures 3 mm in length
(PHOTO COURTESY OF CARMENA AND MAHARBIZ)

what we needed. The physics just weren't there," Carmena recalled. "So we're like, 'I guess that's it!'"[b]

But soon after, Maharbiz had a "eureka" moment—"as weird as it sounds, it occurred to me in a parking lot. You just think about it and all these things align."[c] His idea was to use ultrasound. In comparison to RF, which requires millimeter- or centimeter-sized antennas, ultrasonic energy can be collected with tiny piezocrystals that can be as small as hundreds of microns. Also, RF radiation gets heavily absorbed by the human body and turns into heat. "Ultrasound doesn't do that," Maharbiz said. "You're just Jell-O—it goes right through you."[d]

Their technology, which they named "neural dust," has the potential to advance brain-machine interfaces that can control prosthetics and improve the lives of millions of people suffering from spinal cord injury, stroke, and other disabling conditions.

In 2013 the potential of neural dust led to a Spark Award grant from Berkeley's Bakar Fellows Program (profiled in chapter 3). In a 2013 article about the Bakar program, Maharbiz said, "The funding encourages us to look at processes—to think about experiments that we wouldn't likely be able to pursue with federal research grants. It's helping us look at how to leverage the activity going on in our labs to push commercialization and help people regain movement." In that same article, Carmena said, "The Bakar support has a very interesting effect on us. I've always thought about bringing this technology all the way from the lab to commercialization to help disabled people. But you're busy and have many obligations, and the goal gets pushed back. The Bakar program changed my mindset. We have access to experts who can help us along this route; resources to understand patent issues. You are almost pushed towards a commercial effort. And that can only help in the long run."[e]

Jose Carmena and Michel Maharbiz with graduate student Peter Ledochowitsch (COURTESY OF CARMENA AND MAHARBIZ)

The research team also leveraged Berkeley's Marvell Nanofabrication shared R&D facility (highlighted in chapter 4), the Berkeley Sensor and Actuator Center (a university-industry research program supported by the US National Science Foundation), the Berkeley SkyDeck startup accelerator program (profiled in chapters 3 and 4), and a unique program at Berkeley that enables startups to conduct commercial R&D in a professor's lab (profiled in chapter 4).[f] In a 2014 faculty profile, Maharbiz said, "Berkeley is weirdly special about people collaborating openly. We have a culture of rewarding that kind of interdisciplinary stuff, and that's what I like. I mean I love doing these things."[g]

In 2017, with $1 million in seed funding, Carmena and Maharbiz cofounded Iota Biosciences to commercialize their bioelectronic implantable medical technology.[h] The two professors shared the role of co-CEOs, and Iota licensed the patent rights from Berkeley. Iota raised a $15 million Series A round of funding in 2018 to advance the company's prototypes for eventual human trials. One of the participants in that funding was the venture capital subsidiary of Astellas, a Tokyo-based global pharmaceutical company. A year later, Astellas and Iota established a collaborative R&D agreement to explore new biosensing and treatment measures using Iota's ultrasmall implantable medical technology. Under that collaboration Astellas and Iota jointly designed implantable medical devices and conducted preclinical studies for several diseases with high unmet medical needs.[i]

In 2020, Astellas acquired Iota for $127.6 million plus an additional $176.5 million for potential milestone achievements. Carmena and Maharbiz said about the acquisition: "The partnership between Iota and Astellas allows us to combine our respective strengths to bring revolutionary new approaches to managing and treating diseases that affect hundreds of millions of people across the world. A new era in bioelectronic medicine is dawning and Iota Biosciences, powered by Astellas, will be leading the charge."[j]

Following the acquisition, Iota focused on multiple projects in the Active Class 3 implantable device space, spanning neural to bioelectronic applications. In 2024 the US Food and Drug Administration approved Iota's investigational device exemption for an early feasibility study focused on an implantable device designed to deliver electrical stimulation directly to the bladder wall, inducing contractions that facilitate bladder emptying in individuals impacted by an underactive bladder. ▪

*(notes on next page)*

a. Carmena had a joint appointment with the Helen Wills Neuroscience Institute at UC Berkeley, and Maharbiz had a joint appointment in the UC Berkeley College of Engineering Bioengineering Department.

b. Quoted in Devin Coldewey, "Iota Biosciences Raises $15M to Produce In-body Sensors Smaller Than a Grain of Rice," *TechCrunch*, December 27, 2018, https://techcrunch.com/2018/12/27/iota-biosciences-raises-15m-to-produce-in-body-sensors-smaller-than-a-grain-of-rice.

c. Quoted in Coldewey, "Iota Biosciences Raises $15M to Produce In-body Sensors."

d. Ibid.

e. Michel Maharbiz, Bakar Fellows Program, https://bakarfellows.berkeley.edu/profile/michel-maharbiz/.

f. The unique program is the RIC FLEXIE program. To learn more, see https://ipira.berkeley.edu/flexie.

g. Georgeann Sack, "Faculty Profile: Michel Maharbiz," *Berkeley Science Review*, April 27, 2014, https://berkeleysciencereview.com/article/2014/04/27/faculty-profile-michel-maharbiz.

h. Iota raised $1 million in seed funding from UC Berkeley almuni Coleman Fung and Richard Passov. Michel Maharbiz also cofounded Cortera Neurotech, Tweedle Technologies, Microreactor, Inc.

i. Press release, September 13, 2019, www.astellas.com/en/system/files/news/2020-10/20190913_EG_2.pdf.

j. Quoted in "Astellas to Aqcuire Iota Biosciences," October 15, 2020, www.astellas.com/en/news/16126.

*(continued from page 145)*

field. The Berkeley Changemaker program goes beyond a simple focus on functional "changemaking skills" or co-curricular activities—it delivers a robust curriculum of courses in departments across the campus.

As of 2025, the Changemaker program includes over forty courses taught by over seventy faculty members drawn from more than thirty academic departments in eleven schools and colleges across the campus. On every metric the campus tracks, Berkeley Changemakers are more diverse than the general undergraduate population. Within just five years, the program marked its ten thousandth student enrollment.

Rich Lyons, one of the cofounders and flag-bearers of Berkeley Changemaker, said: "The program codifies an essential part of what Berkeley has always stood for and provides a narrative that the entire campus has rallied behind—humanists and scientists alike."

## Labs for Biotech Startups: QB3 and Bakar Labs

As profiled in chapter 2, QB3 is a research and commercialization institute launched by Governor Gray Davis in 2000 and affiliated with three University of California campuses: Berkeley, San Francisco, and Santa Cruz. At Berkeley, QB3 research is centered at Stanley Hall—a 285,000-square-foot biosciences and bioengineering building that was completely renovated as part of QB3's launch. Regis Kelly was appointed the executive director of QB3 in 2004.[7] He embraced the strategy of fostering entrepreneurship to advance QB3's mission, which included launching biotech startup company incubator labs and support programs, including on the Berkeley campus.

Following the success of QB3's first incubator lab space for startups at UC San Francisco, the first incubator lab space for biotech startups at Berkeley was launched in 2010. Called the QB3 Garage@Berkeley, the 800-square-foot facility located in Stanley Hall has eight wet lab stations. Each station offers bench and desk space as well as network connections. Resident companies share the use of a prep bench with standard lab facilities, along with space for floor-standing equipment such as a refrigerator, freezer, and centrifuge.[8]

---

7. Regis "Reg" B. Kelly was the executive director of QB3 from 2004 to 2022. Prior to that role, he was a neuroscientist and executive vice chancellor at UC San Francisco.

8. In 2022 another UC Berkeley startup incubator lab opened. The Energy

The Bakar BioEnginuity Hub and Bakar Labs in the former Berkeley Art Museum and Pacific Film Archive building

Under a partnership between QB3, UC Berkeley, and a philanthropic foundation, the QB3 incubator concept hugely expanded with the 2021 launching of the Bakar Bio Labs startup accelerator housed in the Bakar BioEnginuity Hub building.[9] Located on the southern border of Berkeley's core campus in the completely renovated building that had formerly housed the Berkeley Art Museum and Pacific Film Archive, Bakar Bio Labs's 92,000 square feet of state-of-the-art lab, office, and meeting space made it the largest university-owned biotech startup incubator in the United States. Any startup, whether from a UC

---

& Biosciences Institute Entrepreneurial Business Incubator (EBI2), offering 2,000 square feet of rentable lab space for startups conducting biological and chemical R&D.

9. The philanthropic organization that parterned with QB3 and Berkeley was the Bakar Foundation.

The Bakar BioEnginuity Hub and Bakar Labs state-of-the-art lab, office, and meeting space

campus or elsewhere, with pre-seed or seed funding can apply for tenancy at Bakar Labs. Applicants pitch at monthly meetings of the tenant selection committee. The committee assesses each applicant's technology, team, market fit, competitive landscape, and benefit to society.

After acceptance into Bakar Bio Labs, tenant startup teams can access a network of corporate affiliates in biotech, pharma, law, banking, and equipment providers.[10] The corporate affiliates and other Bakar Labs partners provide experts for seminars, panels, and networking events that help companies leverage connections and experience—for example, managing intellectual property and negotiating business development partnerships.

10. As of 2024, the corporate affiliates included Abbvie, Agilent, Amgen, Bayer, Beckman-Coulter, Bio-Rad, the BrightEdge Fund of the American Cancer Society, Caribou Biosciences, the Cystic Fibrosis Foundation, Eli Lilly, Genentech, Goodwin, HSBC, Johnson & Johnson, L'Oreal, Newmark, Silicon Valley Bank, ThermoFisher, venBio, and Wilson Sonsini.

The QB3 Workforce Education in Science and Technology (QWEST) program connects tenant companies with undergraduate and graduate students, and QWEST also funds the students to work as R&D interns for the startups. This experience furthers students' education and provides them with career opportunities. In conjunction with the incubator lab resources, QB3 and Bakar Labs staff offer a pipeline of programs to accelerate the process of technology development, startup ideation, fundraising, networking, and company growth. Those programs include the following:

- **Bakar Fellows.** This program (profiled in chapter 3) funds UC Berkeley (and more recently UC San Francisco) faculty to conduct late-stage academic research that has the potential to progress into companies.

- **QB3's Innovation Discovery.** This program identifies promising technologies from the Bakar Fellows (and other researchers) and helps build and mentor a team that can progress a discovery into a company.

- **QB3's Early-Stage Mentoring.** This program pairs together nascent teams from Innovation Discovery (or elsewhere) with mentors and advisors who can refine the technology, the founding team, its market fit, and its communication with investors in order to raise pre-seed or seed funds.

In addition, in 2024, QB3 and Bakar Labs helped establish and partner with BEVC, an independently operated VC firm that invests in, supports, and mentors companies within the Bakar and QB3 community. A considerable portion of BEVC proceeds flow to the Berkeley Foundation and campus.

During the first three years of its operation, the Bakar Labs's forty tenant startups raised more than $650 million in funding and created over three hundred jobs. With revenues from tenant

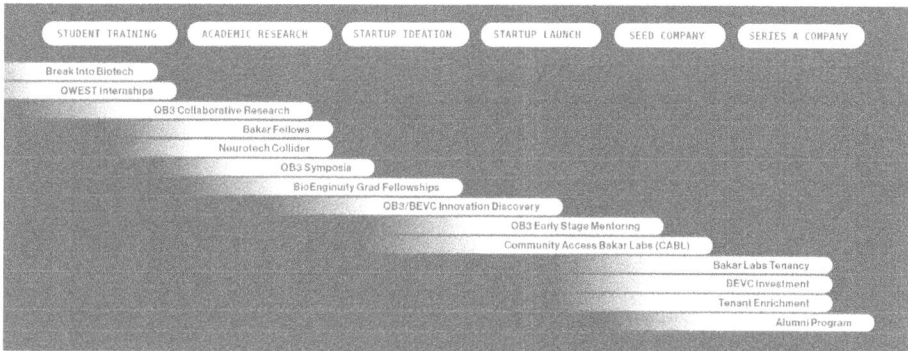

| STUDENT TRAINING | ACADEMIC RESEARCH | STARTUP IDEATION | STARTUP LAUNCH | SEED COMPANY | SERIES A COMPANY |
|---|---|---|---|---|---|

Break Into Biotech
QWEST Internships
QB3 Collaborative Research
Bakar Fellows
Neurotech Collider
QB3 Symposia
BioEnginuity Grad Fellowships
QB3/BEVC Innovation Discovery
QB3 Early Stage Mentoring
Community Access Bakar Labs (CABL)
Bakar Labs Tenancy
BEVC Investment
Tenant Enrichment
Alumni Program

QB3's pipeline of programs address all stages of entrepreneurship and startup journey

rent and corporate affiliates, the QB3 and Bakar Labs budgets are self-sustaining.

As of 2024, Bakar Labs and QB3 continued building on their success. Once again, catalyzed by a generous donor foundation, an energy and materials technology startup company incubator and program (profiled in chapter 6) is targeted for opening in 2028. This initiative—which expands the scope of Bakar Labs and QB3 from human health to planetary health—will offer 146,000 square feet of lab, office, and meeting space to support startups working on energy and materials technology, making it the largest such universityowned facility in the United States. To build momentum for this effort, Bakar Labs launched a pilot incubator facility and programs to foster a critical mass of energy and materials tech companies.

## Building on Biotech I&E Programs: Life Sciences Entrepreneurship Center

One of the challenging goals of UC Berkeley's new CIEO was to increase the capacity of the campus's I&E ecosystem without increasing its complexity and corresponding confusion. The first

Berkeley Life Sciences Entrepreneurship Center

◇◇ Nucleate

## Berkeley LSEC – Nucleate Fellowship

### Jan. 24 – Jul. 1, 2022

Are you interested in a career in biotech entrepreneurship and venture capital?

Berkeley Life Sciences Entrepreneurship Center and Nucleate Bio Bay Area are selecting the second cohort of Fellows to provide hands-on training in **landscaping new technologies** and an introduction to **due diligence and sourcing**.

Independent projects to examine self-chosen 'Target Area' with **mentorship from academic and industry experts**.

**Collaborate** with cohort peers and **network with VCs** to brainstorm through challenges in translating cutting-edge science into new ventures.

For more info, please visit https://lsec.berkeley.edu/fellows or contact lifesciences@berkeley.edu

Program details:

Eligibility: Berkeley PhD students (post-qualifying exam) + postdocs

5 hrs/week * 5.5 months

Stipend provided

ID key factors in early stages of technology development

Apply here by Jan. 31

flagship example of achieving that goal was the 2021 launch of the Life Sciences Entrepreneurship Center (LSEC).[11] As the Berkeley I&E ecosystem's first-of-its-kind "center of centers," LSEC was designed from the ground up to foster life sciences entrepreneurship by building upon (not competing with) existing campus resources. Those other life sciences I&E programs included Bakar Labs, the Innovative Genomics Institute (founded by Berkeley professor and Nobel laureate Jennifer Doudna), QB3, and the Bio Track at the SkyDeck startup accelerator.

Under the leadership of inaugural executive director Darren Cooke, within its first year, LSEC became a first stop for Berkeley's community of life science innovators—from students to postdocs to faculty—interested in the path of moving from concept to company.[12] As of 2024, LSEC supported biotech entrepre-

---

11. The LSEC program was made possible by philanthropic funding from Berkeley alumni Mark and Stephanie Robinson as well as from alumnus and adjunct professor David Kirn and his wife, Kristin Ahlquist.

12. Darren Cooke had previously been a SkyDeck advisor and the head of its life sciences track as well as professional faculty in Berkeley's Haas School of Business. In 2024 he became Berkeley's interim chief innovation and entrepreneurship officer.

**Berkeley** Life Sciences Entrepreneurship Center

**Bio Startup Speed Teaming**
February 17, 4:30-6:45pm, online

Opportunity tailored for:

- Graduate students, postdocs and faculty with a life sciences tech or idea
- Business and other students looking to connect with a startup

Do you have a life sciences startup idea and are looking for a co-founder, collaborator or advisor with complementary skills?

Do you have business or technical skills, but not the technology?

Are you looking for someone to participate with in programs like I-Corps, StEP, SkyDeck, Form+Fund, Nucleate or LAUNCH?

If so, apply to participate in for **Bio Startup Speed Teaming**!

Information and application at: https://lsec.berkeley.edu/speed-teaming

Thank you to our campus partners:

Berkeley IPIRA   HAAS HEALTHCARE ASSOCIATION   qb3

Apply by February 11:

neurship in numerous ways, including the following signature programs: the Nucleate Venture Fellowship, Bio Speed Teaming, and Venture Grants. In 2025, LSEC added an entrepreneurs in residence program to its portfolio of support services.

### Identifying Commercializable Berkeley Technologies: LSEC-Nucleate Venture Fellows Program

LSEC partnered with Nucleate Bay Area in 2021 to launch and run Berkeley's LSEC-Nucleate Venture Fellowship program.[13] The venture fellows selected for this program are innovative Berkeley graduate students and postdoctoral researchers in the life sciences.[14] The program provides fellows with a stipend and a hands-on introduction to performing venture investing–oriented due diligence and innovation sourcing in a life sciences

(continued on page 162)

13. Nucleate is a student-run, stock equity free, nonprofit organization with the goal of facilitating the formation of new life science companies.

14. Tobias Schmid, a 2021 UC Berkeley PhD in neuroscience, was instrumental in establishing and running the LSEC-Nucleate Venture Fellows Program.

## Aduro Biotech: The Fourth Company for a Berkeley Serial Entrepreneur

Stephen Isaacs graduated from UC Berkeley in 1973 with a biochemistry degree. He describes himself back then as a "long-haired, dope-smoking, Sproul Hall window–breaking Vietnam War protestor—sometimes in search of bail money." After a two-year gig as one of the original street vendors on Telegraph Avenue, where he and his girlfriend (now wife of fifty-four years) had a terrarium business, Isaacs returned to the campus to work as a lab assistant in the chemistry department. There he serendipitously met chemistry professor John Hearst, who set Isaacs on his path of a life sciences serial entrepreneur and "semi-respectable public company CEO who has done some good things to make the world a better place."[a]

In Hearst's lab Isaacs worked on small molecules called psoralens. These compounds can prevent DNA and RNA from replicating, effectively "killing" the organism—be it a virus, a bacterium, a fungus, or a eucaryotic cell. Hearst tasked Isaacs with improving the reactivity of the psoralens by synthesizing new derivatives that "worked better"—that is, had higher reactivity with DNA and RNA. Isaacs came up with a superior psoralen. In 1976, Isaacs and his lab collaborators published their

Stephen Isaacs in the 1970s

work in *Biochemistry* and received many requests for improved psoralens, which they distributed freely. Isaacs also developed methods to radiolabel the psoralens so they could be tracked. Berkeley obtained multiple patents on the compounds. The research was done in collaboration with well-known organic chemist and professor Henry Rapoport.

With ongoing requests for compounds and his business experience with terrariums, Isaacs realized that he "could sell these compounds, and we could start a little business." In 1979, that led to Isaacs's second business, HRI Associates, which stood for "Hearst, Rapoport, and Isaacs." Isaacs found some space in a nearby abandoned building (with some very questionable tenants) that Shell Development Company had vacated. He licensed the psoralen patents from Berkeley and managed to secure a radioactive materials license. His girlfriend helped him build a glove box to make custom-synthesized compounds with radioactive tags in specific positions that people would pay a lot of money for. HRI expanded to work with the National Cancer Institute and early biotech companies commercializing PCR (including biotech companies with UC Berkeley roots, such as Cetus and Chiron). However, like the terrariums, HRI's business had limited potential.

In 1989, Isaacs started collaborating with UC San Francisco

Stephen Isaacs in the 1990s

on the pressing issue of blood contaminated with HIV. They realized that Berkeley's patented psoralen technology could kill viruses and bacteria in blood, making it safe for transfusion. That inspired the 1991 launch of the Cerus Corporation, Isaacs's third company.

At the time Baxter was the major manufacturer of blood collection and transfusion equipment. The company was under siege from people getting infected with HIV and "non-A-non-B" hepatitis—now Hepatitis C. Baxter came to Cerus and established a collaboration that ultimately provided more than $100 million in revenues to Cerus. The company went public in 1997 as a Wall Street "darling" and reached a $2 billion valuation by 2000. However, Cerus's business was complicated. It encountered many ups and downs. Nonetheless, as of 2025, Cerus's Intercept Blood Systems is approved in some seventy-five countries and has saved countless lives by preventing transfusion-transmitted diseases.

Isaacs was Cerus's founding CEO for fourteen years, until 2004. While at Cerus, Isaacs became intrigued with other emerging life science technologies, one of which was developed in the lab of Berkeley professor Daniel Portnoy. The technology used proteins typically found on the surface of cancer cells to activate an immune response using T-cells that kill cancer. That led to the 2007 launch of Aduro BioTech, Isaacs's fourth company. Aduro licensed the technology from Berkeley and set out to use a bacterium called *Listeria monocytogenes* to deliver the proteins that would stimulate the anticancer response. Early success in late-stage pancreatic and other types of cancer generated lots of interest. Aduro launched numerous clinical trials and received several multimillion-dollar upfront payments from deals with companies such as Johnson & Johnson for lung and prostate cancer. Unfortunately, Aduro's approach ultimately failed in late-stage trials.

At about the same time, Aduro was also conducting R&D in STING biology based on technology developed in the lab of Berkeley professor Russell Vance. Aduro licensed the patents from Berkeley. In 2015 the company's improvements on the technology led to a $250 million upfront payment from Novartis and an initial public offering a month later with a $3 billion valuation. But, once again, despite all the initial glory and hope, in the end the technology didn't work in late-stage clinical trials—which is an all-too-common outcome in biotech. In 2019, Aduro merged with Chinook Therapeutics, a company with complementary expertise. In 2023, Novartis bought the merged company for $3.5 billion.

Isaacs was Aduro's founding CEO for thirteen years, until 2020. While leading Aduro, he started several initiatives, including the Alliance for Global Health and Science and the Immunotherapeutics and Vaccine Research Initiative, which Aduro supported with about $10 million in research grants. While at Aduro, Isaacs helped launch X-Biotix to address the problem of antimicrobial resistance. He was the company's chairman. In 2021, X-Biotix set out to use the immune system to fight bacteria in a way that can bypass microbial resistance. As of 2025, Isaacs is the chairman and CEO of X-Biotix, which has collaboratively sponsored research agreements with several universities, including eleven faculty at Berkeley in chemistry, immunology, and bacteriology.

Looking back on the societal impact of his long career, Isaacs acknowledges it was all enabled by his scientific education at Berkeley, getting a break from Professor Hearst, and leveraging Berkeley's world-class research enterprise. ▪

a. Quotations throughout this section are taken from an email and presentation that Stephen Isaacs sent to Mike Cohen, February 18, 2025. The presentation is titled "Forty Years of Science and Biotech: A Personal Journey."

area of each fellow's interest, such as synthetic biology, gene therapy, and microfluidics. During the first months of the program, the fellows generate a historical landscape analysis of specific Berkeley research areas to identify patterns of startup formation and success. In the second half of the fellowship, the participants contribute to Berkeley's I&E ecosystem by identifying and analyzing potentially commercializable technologies that could lead to new startups. Many of the program's alumni have gone on to become startup founders and venture capital investors.

### *Matchmaking Berkeley Startup Cofounders: LSEC Bio Startup Speed Teaming*

One of the most common pain points in academic life sciences entrepreneurship is finding a cofounder or advisor with complementary skills, particularly with business expertise. Investors expect balanced startup teams, and several Berkeley entrepreneurship programs require it, such as Berkeley SkyDeck and NSF I-Corps. To address that challenge, LSEC launched in 2022 its Bio Startup Speed Teaming program to help Berkeley-affiliated entrepreneurs find cofounders and advisors with complementary skills and experiences. The program's structure was inspired by pop culture speed-dating events and SkyDeck's method for matching cohort startups with key advisors. Two times per year, the program curated about ten participants from a pool of applicants with expertise in life science technologies and an equal number of participants with business expertise applicable to life science startups. Then, over the course of about a two-hour online session, the tech and biz participants are paired and sent to breakout rooms for ten-minute one-on-one discussions. This program has helped launch the founding teams of several promising startups, such as HOPO Thera-

**LSEC Venture Grant Program**

Berkeley Life Sciences Entrepreneurship Center

Want to launch a bio startup at Berkeley?
*Let us help you build it. Next cohort March 2025 - February 2026*

**Money to Get it Going:**
- $100k R&D grant to promote translation of technology to commercialization
- $200k investment from the Berkeley SkyDeck Fund ($100k+$100k, traunched)

**Built with the Best of Berkeley:**
- Admission to Berkeley SkyDeck: advisors, workshops, investors, huge demo day
- Participation in I-Corps @ LSEC and Bio Startup Speed Teaming
- Presentation to BioEng 153/253: *Biotechnology Entrepreneurship*
- Participation in QB3's SBIR grant-writing workshop
- Optional participation in IP Law Practicum, and Lean Transfer class at Haas

**Outstanding Resources:**
- Showcase event and pitch to experts and investors
- Access to Bakar Labs events and CABL program
- Access to the UC Berkeley Drug Discovery Center

Info and apply by January 24, 2025:
lsec.berkeley.edu/venture-grant

**Eligibility:**
- Academic UC Berkeley teams of at least two members (faculty, PhD students, postdocs, and other graduate students, including business and engineering)
- Life sciences field: therapeutics, diagnostics, medical device, research tools
- Innovation based on Berkeley IP

SKYDECK    Berkeley IPIRA    Bakar Labs    qb3    CORPS

peutics. In 2024, QB3 took over the Bio Startup Speed Teaming program from LSEC and expanded it from some twenty to sixty participants, in the same format.

## Navigating Berkeley's I&E Ecosystem:
## LSEC Venture Grant Program

Berkeley's vast I&E ecosystem has a great deal of resources to offer. But the size and related complexity of the ecosystem can be confusing. LSEC helps aspiring Berkeley entrepreneurs navigate the best pathway through the campus's I&E ecosystem. In addition to providing ad hoc customized advice to Berkeley founders, LSEC launched in 2023 a Venture Grant Program. This program provides $100,000 in grant funding to promising early-stage (pre-seed funding) startups that are commercializing technology developed at Berkeley. The program helps the startups take advantage of Berkeley offerings such as the SkyDeck startup accelerator and the Bakar Labs incubator facility.

## Benefitting from Creating Value for Society: Equity Solutions Services

Startups that have spun out of UC Berkeley based on technology developed on the campus have created huge value for society and generated trillions of dollars in wealth for those who have held stock equity in those companies. Unfortunately the university has had only a minor equity stake in just a fraction of those startups. That has been a lost opportunity for contributing to the funding of Berkeley's research and education mission (especially as funding from the State of California has declined over the past decades).

In 2020 the realization of the magnitude of those lost funding opportunities led to the campus's strategic emphasis on obtaining more stock equity (and future investment participation rights) in startups through Berkeley's license agreements, startup accelerator programs, and other contractual relationships between the campus and startups. To pursue that strategy and maximize Berkeley's financial outcomes, the campus's I&E Office formed the Equity Solutions Services (ESS) team. Under the leadership of its inaugural director Omar Qarshi, ESS manages Berkeley's corporate stock holdings (and associated future investment participation rights) obtained from intellectual property licenses and access to campus accelerator/incubator facilities. The ESS team aims to diversify the types of transactions that support the university's mission and result in university ownership of company equity.

ESS collaborates with stakeholders across the startup equity lifecycle, from company formation to capital raises, and ultimately corporate liquidity events such as mergers, acquisitions, and initial public offerings. In addition to collaborating with programs throughout Berkeley's I&E ecosystem, ESS works with the venture capital funds that are affiliated with the university and share a portion of their investment profits with the campus (profiled in chapter 4).

In 2023, ESS participated in a novel collaboration with several Berkeley offices that conceived a spinout business, recruited the founding team, and helped launch the venture—all in return for substantial equity ownership in the startup Second Lab. That collaboration was the first instance of a venture studio process that the campus plans to replicate.

As of 2025, the ESS team has not only enabled the campus to benefit more substantially from the financial success of startups, it has increased startups' access to investors who have a special interest in the university. Conversely, ESS has increased access to successful startups for investors who are affiliated with Berkeley—a win-win-win for investors, the university, and its entrepreneurs.

## Berkeley Research Infrastructure Commons

One of the biggest challenges for startup companies with R&D-intensive business plans is access to the expensive laboratory facilities required to develop their products. As with many US research universities, UC Berkeley has had a history of enabling the excess capacity of some of its specialized R&D facilities to be shared by for-profit companies (including startups) for fees at commercial rates (not subsidized academic rates). Those fees help universities offset their costs to maintain the expensive facilities. And even at commercial rates, the fees can be within the budgets of startups because it is less expensive to rent on hourly rates (instead of monthly rates) and lease shared space (instead of dedicated space).

However, similar to other universities, Berkeley's shared R&D facilities are decentrally managed by different campus units, and the various facilities-use contracts with companies were fraught with time-consuming negotiations—for example, concerning intellectual property ownership, confidentiality, insurance, liability, and indemnification as well as federal and state compliance requirements. The laborious contracting process impeded companies' use of the shared R&D facilities. That situation worsened during the COVID-19 pandemic's lockdown, when many Berkeley shared R&D facilities spiraled into budget deficits and faced potential shutdowns.

That crisis motivated the campus to develop standard contracts for commercial use of shared R&D facilities that would incorporate the most business-friendly terms that the university could allow. The new standard contracts even incorporated an exception to the university's IP policy to allow companies to have sole ownership of their IP and sole use of their data. Furthermore, the business-friendly contracts were structured so that every Berkeley shared R&D facility could use the same core contract and only need to customize addendums for each facility's fees, contact information, and other content unique to each facility and customer. The result was a contract and process that most companies could e-sign without any negotiations.

Now that the campus had standard, business-friendly contracts and a fast e-signable contracting process that could be used by all of its shared R&D facilities, the campus wanted to promote those improvements to its dozens of shared R&D facilities and to the market—especially startups. To amplify that standardization, the campus created a brand name for all its shared R&D facilities that adopted the standard, called the Berkeley Research Infrastructure Commons (RIC). The Berkeley RIC was piloted in April 2021 and officially launched in July 2021. Berkeley's decentrally managed shared R&D facilities weren't forced to join the RIC, but approval into the RIC was the only way facilities could use the RIC's business-friendly contracts and e-sign process. Instead, shared R&D facilities could voluntarily request to join the RIC by completing a one-page application and receiving approval through a simple campus-wide review process.

As of 2024, twenty-seven R&D facilities have been approved into the Berkeley RIC as listed at ric.berkeley.edu. The Berkeley RIC has become one of the campus's I&E ecosystem strategic assets for entrepreneurs and their startups (as highlighted on this list of Berkeley I&E platforms: iande.berkeley.edu/sites/default/files/4_24_platforms_that_advance_ie_at_ucb.pdf). Data from 2022 indicates that more than 20 percent of companies that use the RIC are startups. Other UC campuses have adopted Berkeley's "open-source version" of the RIC's contracts, contracting process, facilities application and approval process, and also the trademarked Research Infrastructure Commons brand. In 2023, Berkeley spun out a startup named Second Lab to commercialize a cloud-based platform—inspired by the Berkeley RIC—for universities to scale commercial access to their shared R&D facilities. See secondlab.com, for more information.

## Alt Labs: From Alt Student Body to Alt Meat Innovations

Motivated to address the detrimental environmental and health impacts of the meat industry, the rise of leading-edge companies offering plant-based or lab-grown alternatives to animal farming resonated with the ethos of many in the UC Berkeley community. Seizing on that somewhat latent community interest, Berkeley's Sutardja Center for Entrepreneurship and Technology (SCET, profiled in chapter 2) launched in 2019 the Alternative Meat (Alt:Meat) X-Lab course and associated Alt Meat Challenge annual pitch competition. With the tagline "where food technology meets entrepreneurship," the goal of the course and competition has been to cultivate the next generation of food innovators focused on environmentally sustainable, healthy, and delicious foods.

Not surprisingly, Berkeley's diverse student community and inclusive entrepreneurship ethos led to unconventional, out-of-the-box innovations. Rather than focusing solely on mainstream foods such as chicken nuggets, hamburgers, and bacon, which appeal to the mass market palate, the food innovations and startup ideas coming out of Berkeley's Alt:Meat X-Lab have expanded to the tastes of different cultures and ethnicities. Examples include alt pork belly, a key ingredient in many Asian recipes (Bryan Wong spun out Belli Meats), alt sushi-grade tuna for poke bowls (Kelly Pan spun out Impact Food, which partnered with Pokeworks for mass distribution), and a plant-based alternative for crab meat (Kate Sullivan and Pinkie Temcharoem spun out Uncracked).

The creativity generated in the Alt:Meat X-Lab inspired SCET to launch a series of highly experiential Challenge Lab courses in which students form startup teams to create technology solutions that address societal problems.

# SIX

# Ongoing Growth and Alignment with the Mission

Learning and innovation go hand in hand. The arrogance of success is to think that what you did yesterday will be sufficient for tomorrow.

→ WILLIAM POLLARD, American Physicist, Executive Director, Oak Ridge Institute of Nuclear Studies

## Berkeley I&E, 2025 and Beyond

With UC Berkeley's first chief innovation and entrepreneurship officer (CIEO) assuming leadership of the campus as its twelfth chancellor in July 2024, the momentum of I&E at Berkeley and beyond has been brighter than ever. No other Berkeley chancellor has had as deep of a first-hand knowledge of I&E as Chancellor Rich Lyons. As of 2024, university rankings indicated that Berkeley had successfully maintained its preeminence in fundamental research while also establishing leadership in translational research and societal benefit.[1] Campus data indicate that students and faculty are increasingly choosing Berkeley because of their passion for innovation, entrepreneurship, and startups. However, structural financial pressures continued to challenge the campus's comprehensive excellence and capacity building.

---

1. Some thirty Berkeley graduate programs rank in the top ten according to 2024 rankings in *US News and World Report*.

Nonetheless, a pipeline of new I&E capacity-building projects exemplified Berkeley's ongoing I&E expansion. These projects, most profiled in this chapter, include the following:

- **Berkeley Space Center.** This 36-acre innovation hub is located at the NASA Ames Research Center in the heart of Silicon Valley. There, UC Berkeley, in collaboration with NASA and private industry, will identify, incubate, and launch future technological breakthroughs.

- **Bakar Labs.** The new incubator (based on the model of the Bakar Bio Labs) will open in 2028 in a new building on the west side of campus that will provide resources and support to entrepreneurs in energy production and materials technologies.

- **Berkeley Haas Entrepreneurship Hub.** Opened in the spring of 2025, this hub is a home for entrepreneurs and startup teams to exchange ideas and test concepts as well as host club meetings, mentorship activities, and other events. It also provides navigation resources for Berkeley's vast I&E ecosystem.

- **Berkeley Innovation Zone.** This 2-acre site in downtown Berkeley next to the west side of the campus will be home to new research labs and collaborations with industry.

- **The Gateway.** Opening in 2026, the new Gateway, located at the northwest entry point of the Berkeley campus, will be the home of the College of Computing, Data Science, and Society. A next generation factory of ideas, the 367,270-square-foot Gateway will be dedicated to nurturing innovation and collaboration, addressing global challenges by harnessing the power of artificial intelligence, machine learning, and data science for good.

Artistic rendering of the new Gateway (SOURCE: WEISS/MANFREDI)

During a summer 2024 interview Chancellor Lyons was asked, "What is your vision for the future of innovation and entrepreneurship on campus, and how do you plan to support and expand these areas at UC Berkeley?" The chancellor responded, "The picture that's painted in my mind for the future of I&E is one that is tightly linked to, and a strong driver of, our University's mission. The core words of our UC mission statement are 'providing long-term societal benefit.' I&E is a really important way that this happens, across all three of our mission-statement 'hows'—research, teaching, and public service."[2]

While Lyons was CIEO, he sought novel revenue streams for the university that leveraged Berkeley's I&E excellence. As chancellor he has continued to be galvanized by the question, "How

2. "SCET Q&A with Rich Lyons," August 5, 2024, https://scet.berkeley.edu/rich-lyons-the-future-of-innovation-and-entrepreneurship-berkeley/.

does Berkeley participate more in the economic value that it creates in ways that are consistent with its mission and values?"[3] At the conclusion of a September 2024 interview with the chancellor, he said, "The root of our preeminence is fundamental research." He then quoted Clark Kerr, the first chancellor of UC Berkeley: "To what use shall we put it?"

The Berkeley I&E ecosystem, which was embryonic in the twentieth century, nurtured during the early twenty-first century, and exuberant over the past decade, will continue to be *put to use* in the coming decades in ever-changing and world-changing ways.

■ ■ ■ ■ ■

## A Satellite Campus for Innovation: Berkeley Space Center

Throughout the growth of UC Berkeley's I&E ecosystem, practically all its programs have been headquartered on or in close proximity to Berkeley's 178-acre core campus. The campus's borders with the city's commercial and retail neighborhoods have been conducive to programs that bridge academic research with the private sector, such as Berkeley's technology licensing office (profiled in chapter 2), Wireless Research Center, SkyDeck startup accelerator (profiled in chapters 3 and 4), Bakar Bio Labs incubator (profiled in chapter 5), and future Bakar Labs incubator for energy and materials technologies startup companies (profiled in this chapter).

However, the densely built-out neighborhoods surrounding the northern, western, and southern parts of the campus as well as the steep parkland and national laboratory facilities on the eastern edge of the campus have constrained large land-

3. "Kind of a Big Deal," *Haas Newsroom*, Summer 2024, https://newsroom.haas .berkeley.edu/kind-of-a-big-deal/.

intensive I&E opportunities for Berkeley. Accordingly, in 2018 the campus leadership was intrigued with a new opportunity to develop a 15-acre parcel on the expansive Moffett Field site of the NASA Ames Research Center in the heart of Silicon Valley. Led by former UC Regent Darek DeFreece, a Berkeley team assessed the real estate development opportunity, which later expanded to 36 acres (about 20 percent of the size of the core campus) and up to 1.4 million square feet of entitled space. The team envisioned the university collaborating with industry partners to build a mixed-use development of research labs, academic classrooms, and office space, along with complementary retail, short-term stay, and long-term housing.

In 2019 a faculty steering committee led by Gordon Rausser, a former Berkeley professor and dean of the College of Natural Resources, evaluated the viability of the Moffett project under constraints such as no use of public university funds. The final "Rausser Report" outlined opportunities and risks of the development and potential joint initiatives to pursue with Berkeley, NASA, and industry partners. The strategy for implementing the project relied on finding a private master development partner who would enter into a joint venture with Berkeley, obtain third-party capital, and share profits from a successful development, while absorbing the financial risk of an unsuccessful development. After conducting a comprehensive selection process, the campus chose SKS Partners, a firm that had led successful projects at UC San Francisco.

In 2021 a Berkeley team led by DeFreece, chancellor Carol Christ, executive vice chancellor and provost Paul Alivisatos, and vice chancellor of finance Rosemarie Rae received approval by the UC Regents for a seventy-year ground lease at Moffett Field, with extension possibilities for a total of ninety-nine years. In 2022, Berkeley finalized its joint venture agreement with SKS. Under the innovative partnership the university contributed the ground lease it had negotiated with NASA, the Berkeley brand, and the university's global reputation. In return, Berkeley will share equally in the partnership's profits, after payment of the ground lease fees and return on investment for the project's funders. Over time, the development should produce profits to ensure that the site is self-sustaining without using public university funds.

Berkeley deepened its relationship with NASA in 2022 by establishing the Space Act Agreement. Initially encompassing joint workshops and conferences, the agreement also sets the stage for future collaborations spanning science, engineering, and policy. In 2023 the university publicly announced the Moffett project as the Berkeley Space Center led by UC Berkeley professor Alexandre Bayen as its associate provost. The project is expected to break ground in 2026. In the interim the Space Center team has already started fostering collaborations between Berkeley, NASA, and industry partners, including the following:

- An astro-aero industry consortium with Berkeley's Industrial Engineering & Operations Research Department.

- Symposia with NASA in advanced aviation and extreme environments.

- A revamped Air & Space track at Berkeley's SkyDeck accelerator (profiled in chapters 3 and 4) for startups commercializing aviation, aeronautical, and space technology.

- The Berkeley College of Engineering's new aerospace major, which in its first cohort provided more than half the

Artistic rendering of Berkeley Space Center (RENDERING BY FIELD OPERATIONS AND HOK)

students with internships at NASA Ames under the Space Act Agreement.

▪ An Aviation Prize, where teams of undergraduate and graduate students from each of CITRIS's four UC campuses compete to design autonomous vehicle flight corridors between UC campuses and the Berkeley Space Center site at Moffett Field.

As of 2025, the Berkeley Space Center has continued the development of a research industry park focused on deep and transformative technology in fields such as data science, quantum computing, astrobiology, aeronautics and astronautics, and space policy and law.

## Bakar Labs for Energy and Materials Tech Startups

UC Berkeley has more than three hundred faculty in engineering, computer science, chemistry, the physical and life sciences, environmental design, law, policy, business, and other fields that are engaged in energy and materials research.[4] However, the campus lacks sufficient R&D incubation labs and entrepreneurship programs to help startups commercialize Berkeley's energy and materials tech innovations for energy independence, technology leadership, and job creation.

That situation inspired Berkeley to announce in 2024 plans for Bakar Labs for energy and materials, a new facility that will provide Berkeley innovators with the resources they need to launch companies in the burgeoning fields of energy production, materials engineering, advanced batteries, and electrification. Expected to open in 2027, the donor-funded facility will include labs and flexible scale-up space tailored to support a diverse range of R&D, from renewable energy and carbon capture to more efficient building materials and agricultural practices.

Bakar Labs is part of a larger plan to redevelop the west side of Berkeley's campus into a center for life sciences, materials science, and energy and materials research. The project, called the Berkeley Innovation Zone (profiled in this chapter), will include two buildings—the five-story, 145,000-square-foot Bakar Labs building and an additional research facility—along with open space and parking. In a 2024 interview then chancellor Carol Christ said, "The Bakar ClimatEnginuity Hub represents a tremendous opportunity to educate the next generation of climate innovators and support our faculty in bringing their transformative ideas to life. The new facility will support the campus in its mission to address one of society's greatest challenges."

Modeled on the success of Berkeley's Bakar Bio Labs (pro-

---

4. This section is largely sourced from Kara Manke, "Bakar ClimatEnginuity Hub: Berkeley's New Home for Climate Innovation," *UC Berkeley News*, May 16, 2024, https://news.berkeley.edu/2024/05/16/bakar-climatenginuity-hub -berkeleys-new-home-for-climate-innovation/.

Artistic rendering of the new Bakar Labs building (RENDERING BY GENSLER)

filed in chapter 5), the new Bakar Labs building will support up to seventy-five startups with programs that build community and facilitate connections to industry partners and investors. In support of the university's educational mission, programs will also offer internships and fellowships that will train undergraduate and graduate students to become future leaders in energy and materials innovation. "Our university excels at basic discovery, innovation, and policy," said David Schaffer, a Berkeley chemical and biomolecular engineering professor who is the inaugural director of the new Bakar Labs program in energy and materials tech. "Translating basic academic discoveries into companies that scale them into products can broadly benefit society and really change the world."

Before the building opens, Bakar Labs is building momentum by launching a pilot energy and materials incubator housed at Bakar Bio Labs and other campus spaces. The pilot is building a pipeline of talent through mentorship and student internships as well as early engagement of investor networks and industry affiliates to accelerate a number of startups that will move into the new building once it's complete. "Human health and planetary health are two of the major challenges facing our society," said Schaffer, who directs QB3 as well as Bakar Labs (which now comprises Bakar Bio Labs and the new building and program for energy and materials). "Our human health incubator and programs, Bakar Bio Labs, is really off to the races, and we're thrilled to now have the opportunity to take on this other major societal problem."

## A Convening Home for Students: Berkeley Haas Entrepreneurship Hub

For students who are interested in entrepreneurship or "entrepre-curious," taking advantage of UC Berkeley's vast I&E ecosystem can be daunting and confusing. That problem inspired the launch of the campus's Entrepreneurship Hub (eHub) in November 2024. eHub's purpose is to make entrepreneurship easier and more accessible for everyone, and eHub's navigator staff person is at the center of that mission. The navigator is the in-person connector to I&E resources across the campus. The navigator is like a concierge to Berkeley's online gateway to I&E, begin.berkeley.edu (profiled in chapter 4).

eHub has a three-segment program that helps students

(1) identify meaningful problems aligned with their passions, (2) validate and delve deeper into those problems, and (3) build and test solutions that address validated problems. Finally, eHub hosts events that enable student entrepreneurs to build community, brainstorm on opportunities, and find cofounders.

Artistic rendering of Berkeley's eHub housed in a renovated building originally designed by Berkeley alumna Julia Morgan

## Interconnecting Industry and Research: Berkeley Innovation Zone

In 2023, UC Berkeley unveiled a plan to develop what it characterizes as an Innovation Zone on a nearly 2-acre city block in downtown Berkeley adjacent to the western edge of the core campus. The zone will include two new buildings totaling about 486,000 square feet—with academic research and collaboration space, parking, and open space.

One of the buildings is the new Bakar Labs facility (profiled in this chapter) that will provide wet labs and flexible scale-up space for campus faculty, researchers, and campus-affiliated entrepreneurs to incubate startup companies that provide solutions for renewable energy and related challenges.

The Innovation Zone is intended to deepen the university's foothold in entrepreneurship and startups by advancing research discoveries into beneficial, scalable businesses. "It's going to connect to our science very, very deeply in several key

The future location and layout of UC Berkeley's Innovation Zone (TOP: IMAGE BY GOOGLE SATELLITE; BOTTOM SOURCE: DGA + WIESS/MANFREDI)

areas for society," said Rich Lyons, UC Berkeley's former chief innovation officer and subsequent chancellor.[5]

5. "'Innovation Zone' Is Coming to Downtown Berkeley," Bakar Bio Labs, https://bakarlabs.berkeley.edu/innovation-zone-is-coming-to-downtown -berkeley/.

# SEVEN

# Strategic Conclusions

UC Berkeley's transformation into an I&E powerhouse was improbable. This public university campus faced significant challenges, including a foundational disdain for involvement with commercial activities, a shared-governance structure that limits centralized top-down control, and declining state funding. Yet those challenges shaped Berkeley's path to I&E excellence. This chapter summarizes Berkeley's I&E ascendance and provides strategic takeaways that can inform other universities in building and elevating their I&E ecosystems to reach their full potential.

## How Berkeley Transformed into an I&E Powerhouse

Two seminal attributes of UC Berkeley made it unlikely to become an entrepreneurship and startup leader. First, Berkeley's founding in 1868 as a land grant institution and constitutionally designated public trust led to a general campus disdain for involvement in commercial endeavors. That foundational attitude was exemplified by the mindset that any financial gains from faculty research should accrue to the state and the university, not the inventors, because taxpayers paid their salaries. Second, Berkeley has a tradition of robust shared governance, under which faculty share responsibility for guiding the campus's management. Accordingly, many operational decisions are decentralized among Berkeley's committees, colleges, schools, departments, and even at the faculty level. A central authority at Berkeley, such as the chancellor, did not and could not mandate a campus-wide plan to become an I&E powerhouse.

Despite those two foundational attributes, the following six dynamics eventually upended the campus's norms and made Berkeley an I&E star.

1. Starting in the 1960s and 1970s, pockets of Berkeley faculty and students were at the forefront of digital technology and biotechnology research. Innovations from their research were conducive to the emerging growth of startup company formation and venture capital investment. The early success stories of entrepreneurs and their startups inspired cadres of Berkeley faculty and students to found companies and incubate an I&E culture. The embryonic I&E culture conflicted with the university's norms. However, the culture's intentionally low profile and the campus's decentralized management kept that I&E culture from being drummed out of the campus before it could gain momentum.

2. The Berkeley campus is located in the San Francisco Bay Area. That region, particularly what became known as Silicon Valley, emerged as a leading cluster for startups and entrepreneurship. Berkeley's commutable distance (albeit a lengthy commute) to Silicon Valley helped foster the campus's nascent I&E culture. Many of Berkeley's digital tech and biotech graduates stayed in the metro area of the campus to work and live. An increasing number of those local Berkeley alumni who were successful entrepreneurs hired subsequent Berkeley graduates and maintained relationships with their Berkeley professors. Those interactions bolstered their alma mater's I&E culture.

3. Starting around the turn of this century, reductions in California government funding strained the University of California's budget. Those strains compelled state and university leaders to pursue collaborations with corporations as a source of university funding, resulting in the launch of QB3 and CITRIS (both profiled in chapter 2). Berkeley's embrace of corporate relationships expanded to also legitimize the campus's growing activities with startup companies.

4. Starting around 2007, a realization gained momentum in Berkeley's STEM community that I&E could help the campus address societal problems, such as climate change and human disease. Also a consensus emerged that I&E enhanced students' experiential learning opportunities. That realization and consensus made I&E a campus imperative and catalyzed philanthropic donations to support I&E, such as SCET (profiled in chapter 2) and the Bakar Fellows Program (profiled in chapter 3).

5. By 2013 a culture that valued the passion of entrepreneurs and the excitement of startups spread across Berkeley's STEM community and led to the creation of numerous I&E programs. And by 2018 another consensus emerged that a broadened mindset about entrepreneurship—beyond starting for-profit ventures—benefited students across the entire campus community, including in the humanities and social sciences. That led to the Berkeley Changemaker program (profiled in chapter 5). I&E was not only an imperative, it had become mainstream on the Berkeley campus—driven by faculty, students, and staff alike.

6. In 2024, Berkeley's newly appointed twelfth chancellor extolled a vision of how I&E is instrumental to the university's public mission by maximizing the societal

benefits of Berkeley's discoveries and innovations, and
I&E in the service of the university's tripartite mission can
complement (not displace) the campus's preeminence in
research. That vision exemplified how I&E had become core
to Berkeley's ethos and its future.

## Strategic Takeaways for Pursuing I&E Excellence

The I&E potential of each university varies depending on a campus's inherent attributes. Accordingly, there isn't a simple or for-
mulaic approach to achieving a university's full I&E potential.
Nonetheless, the takeaways highlighted in this section are applicable to most research universities because, with the exception
of the opportunities for local I&E partnerships (#6 below), the
takeaways don't rely on specific attributes (such as proximity to
a regional innovation economy).

### Strategies for Building University I&E Ecosystems

1. **Cultivate a campus culture that values I&E.** At most
   research universities I&E culture starts with STEM faculty.
   That I&E culture spreads to students when professors
   role-model the culture for students and foster students'
   entrepreneurship ambitions. The I&E culture expands to
   campus executives via faculty promotions into administrative leadership positions. Students also influence campus
   I&E culture, especially to the extent that faculty respond
   to student interests (such as a groundswell of interest in
   entrepreneurship). However, student influence on culture
   can be fleeting due to their graduation cycles—unless the
   university's region has attributes that encourage graduates
   to stay to work and live in the metro area of the university

(see strategic conclusion #6 below).

Faculty I&E culture doesn't need to be, nor is it expected to be, pervasive across a campus. However, under a broadened definition of entrepreneurship, I&E culture can be inclusive across the campus community (see strategic conclusion #4 below) and not distort the complementary priorities of fundamental research (see strategic conclusion #7 below) and teaching.

At UC Berkeley, from the 1960s through the 1990s, faculty I&E culture incubated in the chemistry-related departments, the business school, and especially the EECS department. By 2013 that I&E culture had spread throughout the campus's STEM community. The I&E culture expanded to the campus's executive leadership in 2015, when Berkeley professor (and serial entrepreneur) Paul Alivisatos was appointed as vice chancellor for research. Alivisatos was subsequently promoted to executive vice chancellor and provost, and the two following vice chancellors for research were faculty in EECS, Berkeley's most entrepreneurship-oriented department. Berkeley's I&E culture reached another milestone in 2019, when Berkeley professor (and former dean of the School of Business) Rich Lyons was appointed the campus's first chief innovation and entrepreneurship officer and, five years later, became Berkeley's twelfth chancellor.

2. **Build an infrastructure of resources for I&E.** The infrastructure includes (1) curricula about entrepreneurship and startups (including lab-to-market courses that provide experiential learning), (2) startup accelerators, (3) incubator labs, (4) makerspaces, (5) funding for proof-of-concept / translational research, (6) groups of startup investors and

advisors (especially alumni who are experienced entrepreneurs) willing to engage with the campus, (7) networks of faculty and student entrepreneurs, and (8) entrepreneurship events such as pitch competitions, hackathons, and student club gatherings. The ecosystem should encompass the entire entrepreneurship journey, including ideation, incubation, acceleration, and scaling. It should also span startup sectors such as information technology, biotechnology, and social (nonprofit) ventures.

At UC Berkeley students, faculty, and staff have the agency to establish I&E programs independently. Starting around 2013, that autonomy and a spreading I&E culture drove an uncoordinated surge in campus I&E programs. Within five years, at least one Berkeley I&E program existed for every phase of a startup journey and across multiple industry sectors. Those programs were integrated into the curricula (such as the SCET and Cleantech to Market courses) and extracurricular activities (such as Big Ideas and SkyDeck). In 2019, Berkeley's first chief innovation and entrepreneurship officer and his team pursued strategies to harmonize the campus's sprawling I&E ecosystem while continuing to build its capacity. One key example of that strategy was building I&E platforms (not just I&E programs) that multiple campus units could leverage.

3. **Refine I&E-related practices and expertise.** These practices and expertise include collaborations with companies—especially startups—on R&D funding (via, for example, SBIR and STTR US government grants), industry R&D consortia, IP licensing, equity ownership, conflict of interest oversight, shared use of R&D facilities, and, in general, commercializing innovations developed on campus.

In 2004, UC Berkeley established the Industry Alliances Office (IAO), a team with the expertise to negotiate research collaborations with companies (individually and in the form of industry consortia). To expand the campus's opportunities to collaborate with companies, the IAO and Berkeley's Office of Technology Licensing were reorganized under the newly formed Office of Intellectual Property and Industry Research Alliances. That office was promoted as a "one-stop shop" for companies to collaborate with Berkeley on research and the commercialization of innovations from the campus's research. The reorganization set the campus on a trajectory of ongoing refinement to its expertise in company-funded research, IP licensing, startup equity management, conflict of interest oversight, and other I&E-related activities.

### Strategies for Advancing University I&E from Good to Great

4. **Align university leadership with campus I&E culture.** This alignment is achieved when campus executive leaders go beyond supporting I&E to championing it and officially recognizing I&E in faculty appointments and promotions.

   In 2007, UC Berkeley's chancellor and the Lawrence Berkeley National Lab's director cofounded the East Bay Green Corridor, a regional partnership with a mission that included cleantech I&E. In 2012 the deans of the College of Engineering and the School of Business along with the vice chancellor for research launched the SkyDeck startup accelerator. In 2018, Berkeley leadership acknowledged that I&E would be considered in faculty appointments and promotions, and in 2024 the University of California's ten-campus system officially updated its policy. An executive leadership team that championed I&E reached a culminating milestone in 2024 when Berkeley's first chief innovation and entrepreneurship officer was appointed Berkeley's twelfth chancellor.

5. **Make I&E inclusive by broadening its mindset to make it relevant to the entire campus community.** I&E diversity and inclusiveness are facilitated by broadening the definition of entrepreneurship beyond starting for-profit ventures to pursuing high-impact, socially-beneficial ventures and life opportunities.

   In 2018 a UC Berkeley faculty-led report recommended expanding the concept of entrepreneurship so that the benefits of its mindset could be applied across the campus, including in the humanities and social sciences. That recommendation inspired the campus to launch, in 2020, the Berkeley Changemaker, a certificate program that offers more than forty courses based on three throughlines: critical thinking, communication, and collaboration. Changemaker courses have become some of Berkeley's most popular, which shows how an entrepreneurial mindset is mainstream throughout the campus community. The 2024 launch of the Berkeley Haas Entrepreneurship Hub (eHub) further builds upon this ethos.

6. **Establish I&E partnerships with local governments, nearby R&D-intensive organizations, and real estate developers.** Those local partnerships can enable universities to become vortexes for growing a supercritical mass of local human talent—a key attribute of the world's most productive I&E ecosystems. That attribute drives I&E productivity because of the fundamental importance of deep and broad talent (across science, engineering, manufacturing, management, marketing, finance, law, etc). Also, the talent pool's geo-

graphical proximity to the campus maximizes the interpersonal relationships (especially with alumni) and associated serendipitous interactions that often lead to cofounding startups and scaling them. Year after year, universities attract and build human talent. If a university's local region can provide attributes to retain much of that human talent when those people graduate, universities and their regions can grow massive innovation economies.

In 2009, UC Berkeley cofounded the Berkeley Startup Cluster (BSC) with the City of Berkeley Office of Economic Development, the Berkeley Chamber of Commerce, the Downtown Berkeley Association, and the Lawrence Berkeley National Lab. The BSC's initial mission was to slow "innovation drain" by helping spinout companies from the campus and national lab to locate and grow in Berkeley—instead of about fifty miles away in Silicon Valley. By 2023 the BSC had identified about four hundred innovation companies (including startups and R&D-intensive established corporations) with addresses in Berkeley.

In 2021 the Bakar BioEnginuity Hub building opened on the southern edge of Berkeley's core campus. The building houses Bakar Bio Labs—92,000 square feet of state-of-the-art lab, office, and meeting space, including incubator facilities for dozens of biotech startup companies. Under a similar model, in 2028 the new Bakar Labs facility is expected to open on the western edge of Berkeley's campus, and its cutting-edge space and programs will host and support dozens of energy and materials tech startups.

At the onset of 2024 the BSC updated its land use vision and roadmap in recognition that the city's I&E ecosystem (including its variety of office and lab space such as Bakar Bio Labs and the new Bakar Labs facility) was nearing an inflection point. Various R&D-oriented real estate projects were under way that when viewed holistically and combined with Berkeley's existing innovation assets, could elevate the city's status into a world-class cluster for innovation and startups (distinct from but synergistic with the university's I&E stature).

7. **Manage I&E to complement fundamental research.** As with all large, complex organizations, universities must prioritize resources to excel in their mission. Accordingly, universities should manage any expanding capacity for translational research and societal benefit such that the expansion complements (instead of displaces) fundamental research. I&E can flow from and stimulate fundamental research. Universities with robust I&E ecosystems must manage this dynamic because fundamental research and quality teaching are critical to fostering an I&E ecosystem that continually reinvents itself to address the shifting needs of our rapidly changing world.

At UC Berkeley, leaders in academic research—such as professors David Schaffer, Jennifer Doudna, Jay Keasling, Amy Herr, and Paul Alivisatos—have noted how their labs' engagement with entrepreneurship have enriched their scholarly research. Rich Lyons—Berkeley's current chancellor and strong advocate of university I&E—expressed the importance of unwavering support for fundamental research when he said in a September 2024 campus interview, "The world knows about Berkeley because of the fundamental research we do.... And we forget that at our peril."

For more insights about UC Berkeley's I&E ecosystem, visit startupcampus.berkeley.edu.

# CONTRIBUTORS

Launching and growing companies requires the determination and skill of founders, teams of employees, advisors, and investors, as well as an ecosystem of resources. Similarly, launching and publishing this book took determination, skill, and teamwork from a community of people, listed below in alphabetical order.

Mike Alvarez Cohen, Author

Pieter Abbeel

Eric John Abrahamson

Alonzo Addison

Robert Albo

Lisa Alvarez-Cohen

Rachel Barley

Brittney Byrd

Michael Caplan

Jose Carmena

Sibyl Chen

Dylan Chiu

Elizabeth Redman Cleveland

Mike Alvarez Cohen

Darren Cooke

Camille Crittenden

Darek DeFreece

Phillip Denny

Jay Dillon

Diane Dwyer

Jerry Engel

Jill Finlayson

Lee Fleming

Natalee Gibson

Eric Giegerich

Shannelle Glocker

Nicolas Gold

Ken Goldberg

Laura Paxton Hassner

Rachel Haurwitz

Stephen Hills

Steven Horowitz

Stephen Isaacs

Wesley Jackson
Randy Howard Katz
Homayoon Kazerooni
Jay Keasling
Regis Kelly
Craig Kennedy
Camille LeBlanc
Matt Levin
Tsu-Jae King Liu
Diana Lizarraga
Jeffrey Long
Rich Lyons
Michel Maharbiz
Olivier Marie
James Mastalerz
Keith Joseph McAleer
Maryanne McCormick
Jon Metzler
Carol Mimura
Dan Mogulof
Kaspar Mossman
Marty Nemko
Scott Newman
David Peattie
Omar Qarshi

Grant Ricketts
David Riemer
Andy Ross
David Schaffer
Julia Schaletzky
Gino Segre
Curt Setzer
Laleh Shayesteh
Rhonda Shrader
Ken Singer
Matthew Sonsini
Lizi Sprague
Laura Stachel
Debra Summers
Naresh Sunkara
Ken Sunshine
David Teece
Robert Tjian
Erich van Rijn
Colleen Rovetti
Robert Vogel
Kate Warne
Caroline Winnett
Ming Wu

# INDEX

*Page numbers with f indicate a figure or photo.*

MIKE ALVAREZ COHEN is the principal author of *Startup Campus*. For over a decade, Mike has been involved with UC Berkeley's transformation into an entrepreneurship powerhouse through his role as Director of Innovation Ecosystem Development at the campus.

In February 2024, while Rich Lyons was UC Berkeley's inaugural Chief Innovation and Entrepreneurship Officer, he co-launched the *Startup Campus* project with Mike and Laura Hassner, who was at that time Executive Director for Innovation, Entrepreneurship, and the Berkeley Changemaker program. When Rich became Chancellor in July 2024, Mike and Laura expanded the book project's core leadership team to include Darren Cooke, who succeeded Rich as Berkeley's Chief Innovation and Entrepreneurship Officer.

Mike, Laura, and Darren planned and implemented the book project in collaboration with dozens of Berkeley faculty, alumni, and staff—many of whom are members of the campus's 100-person-strong Innovation and Entrepreneurship Council. The result was a campus-wide team effort over 1.5 years to tell the story of how UC Berkeley emerged as an unexpected leader in entrepreneurship and startups.

*Startup Campus* has been entirely funded by philanthropy, and all proceeds from book sales support research, education, and entrepreneurship at Berkeley.